Simple Friendships II

14 Fabulous Quilts from Blocks Stitched among Friends

Kim Diehl and Jo Morton

Martingale®
Create with Confidence

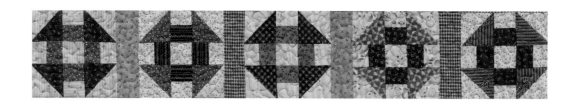

Simple Friendships II:
14 Fabulous Quilts from Blocks Stitched among Friends
© 2019 by Kim Diehl and Jo Morton

Martingale®
19021 120th Ave. NE, Ste. 102
Bothell, WA 98011-9511 USA
ShopMartingale.com

Printed in China
24 23 22 21 20 19   8 7 6 5 4 3 2 1

Library of Congress Cataloging-in-Publication Data is available upon request.

ISBN: 978-1-60468-979-2

MISSION STATEMENT

We empower makers who use fabric and yarn to make life more enjoyable.

CREDITS

PUBLISHER AND
CHIEF VISIONARY OFFICER
Jennifer Erbe Keltner

CONTENT DIRECTOR
Karen Costello Soltys

MANAGING EDITOR
Tina Cook

ACQUISITIONS EDITOR
Amelia Johanson

COPY EDITOR
Jennifer Hornsby

DESIGN MANAGER
Adrienne Smitke

COVER AND
INTERIOR DESIGNER
Regina Girard

STUDIO PHOTOGRAPHER
Brent Kane

LOCATION PHOTOGRAPHER
Adam Albright

ILLUSTRATOR
Missy Shepler

SPECIAL THANKS

Photography for this book was taken at the home of Julie Smiley of Des Moines, Iowa, and at the Garden Barn in Indianola, Iowa.

Contents

Greetings from Jo and Kim!

If you love fabric and patchwork, making memories with friends, and stitching it all together into a treasured quilt, can there ever be too much of a good thing? We don't think so! In fact, we so enjoyed blending ideas and piecing blocks for our first round of Simple Friendships quilts, we decided to double down and do it all again.

With so many block choices to consider, and not nearly enough time to make them all, we tossed around tons of ideas and sifted through scads of possibilities. Finally, with no arm wrestling whatsoever and not even one game of rock-paper-scissors, we agreed upon six tried-and-true blocks that we both absolutely love. From the humble Churn Dash block to sparkling Ohio Stars (because let's be honest, we're all softies when it comes to stars), and even "fancier" blocks like Flock of Geese and Hearth and Home, we were so excited about the creative possibilities that we couldn't wait to begin designing and stitching.

As we worked on our quilts and the designs grew and evolved, we decided to really be true to ourselves and embrace our signature styles. This means that for each featured block you'll find two very different quilts. Our goal is to entice you to gather your favorite prints and start stitching, and we truly hope that we've hit it out of the park and succeeded!

For those of you who enjoy participating in exchanges, you'll find great tips and tidbits of advice in the form of "Swap Talk" boxes at the beginning of each project. If your plan is to enjoy the quiltmaking steps from start to finish in the comfort of your own sewing room while binge-watching your favorite guilty-pleasure TV shows (hey, no judgment here—we do the same thing!), we hope you'll still enjoy reading the tips as you dive into your project.

Our wish is to inspire your creativity, build and strengthen treasured friendships that will last a lifetime, and share your journey as you stitch your beautiful quilts.

Cream of the Crop

Because of its simplicity and charm, as well as the endless design possibilities it brings, the Churn Dash block has long been favored by quiltmakers. Humble yet elegant, this unassuming patchwork block is truly timeless and classic, destined to be loved by generations to come.

~ Kim

SWAP TALK

For this little patchwork quilt, I opted for a fresh take on the tried-and-true Churn Dash block by reversing the traditional placement of the light and dark prints. What I love most about this project is that it's charm-square friendly, making it an ideal choice for incorporating fabrics straight from your stash. I suggest choosing an assortment of medium and dark prints for the blocks and then pairing them with prints in soft shades of cream (not white, which can look a bit stark when mingled with the darker prints). Your finished quilts will sparkle.

Materials

Yardage is based on 42" of usable fabric width after prewashing and removing selvages. Fat quarters are 18" × 21", fat eighths are 9" × 21", chubby sixteenths are 9" × 10½", and charm squares are 5" × 5".

25 charm squares of assorted medium and dark prints (collectively referred to as "dark") OR approximately ⅔ yard *total* of assorted print scraps for Churn Dash blocks*

25 charm squares of assorted cream prints OR approximately ⅔ yard *total* of assorted cream print scraps for Churn Dash blocks

1 fat eighth of tan print for inner border

18 charm squares of assorted medium and dark prints (collectively referred to as "dark") OR approximately ⅝ yard *total* for sashing squares and outer border

10 chubby sixteenths of assorted medium and dark prints for sashing and outer border

1 fat quarter of black print (or color of your choice) for binding

⅞ yard of fabric for backing

31" × 31" square of batting

*For any obviously directional prints, I suggest replacing the 5" charm squares with 6½" squares, as this will give you the ability to cut the patchwork pieces with the print positioned uniformly.

From _1_ cream print charm square, cut:
1 rectangle, 1⅞" × 5"; crosscut into 2 squares,
    1⅞" × 1⅞" (combined total of 50)
2 rectangles, 1" × 5"; crosscut into 4 rectangles,
    1" × 1½" (combined total of 100)

* If you're using a directional print 6½" square, the
1" × 1½" rectangle noted here can be cut with the
remaining three 1" × 1½" rectangles listed below for a
total of four rectangles cut from one 1" × 6½" strip.

Additional Cutting to Complete the Quilt

Cut all pieces across the width of the fabric in the
order given unless otherwise noted.

**From _each_ of the 18 assorted dark print charm
squares for outer border, cut:**
9 squares, 1½" × 1½" (combined total of 162)

**From _each_ of the 10 assorted dark print chubby
sixteenths, cut:**
9 rectangles, 1½" × 3½" (combined total of 90),
    and 2 squares, 1½" × 1½" (combined total of
    20). Combine the 20 squares cut here with
    the previously cut 162 squares, for a grand
    total of 182 assorted print squares.

From the tan print fat eighth, cut:
2 strips, 1" × 19½"
4 strips, 1" × 21"; crosscut _each_ strip into 1 strip,
    1" × 14" (total of 4), and 1 rectangle, 1" × 3½"
    (total of 4)

From the binding print, cut:
6 strips, 2½" × 21" (For Kim's Chubby Binding
    method on page 127, reduce the strip width
    to 2".)

Cutting

You'll need 25 Churn Dash blocks to complete the
featured quilt. Cutting is given for one block at
a time; the number of pieces listed in parentheses
provides the total amount needed to make 25 blocks.
For greater ease in piecing the blocks, keep the pieces
for each block grouped together as you cut them.

    To make this quilt on your own without
swapping blocks, see "Cutting and Piecing . . .
Simplified" on page 9.

Cutting for 1 Churn Dash Block

From _1_ dark print charm square, cut:
1 rectangle, 1⅞" × 5"; crosscut into 2 squares,
    1⅞" × 1⅞" (combined total of 50)
1 rectangle, 1½" × 5"; crosscut into:
    1 square, 1½" × 1½" (combined total of 25)
    1 rectangle, 1" × 1½" (combined total of 25)*
1 rectangle, 1" × 5"; crosscut into 3 rectangles,
    1" × 1½" (combined total of 75)*

Cutting and Piecing . . . Simplified

If you've opted to make this quilt on your own without participating in a block swap, here are a couple of quick tips for efficient cutting and piecing while embracing the scrappy style of this project.

❊ For the cutting steps, build stacks of the assorted medium and dark print charm squares on your ironing surface, with each stack approximately five to six layers deep. I suggest pressing the stack with the addition of each new print to help anchor the layers firmly together for easier cutting.

❊ If your fabric mix includes stripes, plaids, or prints with a pronounced grid, I suggest placing these prints as the top layer of each stack to ensure the lines remain straight and true as you cut. Repeat this step using the assorted cream charm squares. Next, separate the cut patchwork pieces, grouping them together by print. Last, pair each grouped set of dark pieces with a complementary set of cream pieces.

❊ To prepare and organize the patchwork for stitching, I like to lay out the pieces for one block onto a paper plate, layer the pieces for an additional block on top, and continue until I've built a stack of layered pieces for six blocks. Once all the blocks have been layered onto paper plates in groups of six, I follow the block directions to work through the stacked patchwork pieces on each plate. These simple steps make it easy to stay organized and help streamline the stitching process.

Finished quilt size: 26½" × 26½" • **Finished block size:** 3" × 3"

Designed by Kim Diehl. Pieced by Jennifer Martinez and Kim Diehl.
Machine quilted by Rebecca Silbaugh.

Piecing for 1 Churn Dash Block

The steps that follow will make 1 block. Repeat these steps to make 25 blocks. Sew all pieces with right sides together using a ¼" seam allowance unless otherwise noted. Press the seam allowances as indicated by the arrows or as otherwise specified.

1. Select a set of dark and cream pieces cut for one block. Use a pencil and an acrylic ruler to draw a diagonal sewing line from corner to corner on the wrong side of each cream 1⅞" square.

2. Layer a prepared cream 1⅞" square onto each dark 1⅞" square. Stitch each pair of layered squares ¼" from each side of the drawn line. Cut each stitched pair in half on the drawn line to make a total of four half-square-triangle units measuring 1½" square, including the seam allowances. Press. Trim away the dog-ear points.

Make 4 units,
1½" x 1½".

3. Join the dark print and cream print 1" × 1½" rectangles in pairs along the long edges to make a total of four pieced squares. Press.

Make 4 units,
1½" x 1½".

4. Lay out four half-square-triangle units, four pieced squares, and one dark 1½" square in three horizontal rows. Join the pieces in each row. Press. Join the rows. Press. The block should measure 3½" square, including the seam allowances.

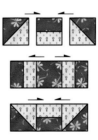

Churn Dash block,
3½" x 3½"

5. Repeat steps 1–4 to make a total of 25 Churn Dash blocks.

Piecing the Quilt Center

1. Lay out five Churn Dash blocks and four assorted print 1½" × 3½" rectangles in alternating positions. Join the pieces. Press. Repeat to make a total of five A rows, measuring 3½" × 19½", including the seam allowances.

Row A.
Make 5 rows, 3½" x 19½".

2. Lay out five assorted 1½" × 3½" rectangles and four assorted 1½" squares in alternating positions. Join the pieces. Press. Repeat to make a total of four B rows, measuring 1½" × 19½", including the seam allowances.

Row B.
Make 4 rows, 1½" x 19½".

3. Lay out the A and B rows in alternating positions. Join the rows. Press the seam allowances toward the B rows. The pieced quilt center should now measure 19½" square, including the seam allowances.

Adding the Borders

1. Join a tan 1" × 19½" strip to the right and left sides of the quilt center. Press the seam allowances toward the tan strips.

2. Selecting the prints randomly, join three dark 1½" squares end to end. Press. Repeat to make a total of 36 units measuring 1½" × 3½", including the seam allowances.

Make 36 units,
1½" x 3½".

3. Selecting the prints randomly, lay out nine dark 1½" squares in three horizontal rows of three squares. Join the squares in each row. Press. Join the rows. Press. Repeat to make a total of four Nine Patch blocks measuring 3½" square, including the seam allowances. (You'll have 22 leftover 1½" squares.)

Make 4 blocks,
3½" x 3½".

4. Lay out 10 assorted dark 1½" × 3½" rectangles and nine pieced units from step 2 in alternating positions. Join the pieces. Press. Repeat to make a total of four outer borders measuring 3½" × 19½", including

the seam allowances. (You'll have 10 leftover rectangles.)

Make 4 pieced outer borders,
3½" x 19½".

5. Join a pieced outer border to the right and left sides of the quilt top. Press the seam allowances toward the inner borders.

6. Join two tan 1" × 14" strips along the short ends. Press the seam allowances open. Measure the width of your quilt top, which should be 26½", and trim the strip to this measurement. Make two. Join these tan strips to the top and bottom edges of the quilt top. Press the seam allowances toward the tan strips.

7. Referring to the pictured quilt on page 10, lay out two Nine Patch blocks from step 3, two tan 1" × 3½" rectangles, and one pieced outer border from step 4. Join the pieces. Press. Repeat to make a total of two pieced border units measuring 3½" × 26½", including the seam allowances. Join these borders to the remaining sides of the quilt top.

Completing the Quilt

Layer and baste the quilt top, batting, and backing. Quilt the layers. The featured quilt was machine quilted with a diamond grid pattern, as shown in the detail photo on page 11. Referring to "Kim's Chubby Binding" method on page 127, or substituting your own favorite method, use the binding strips to bind the quilt.

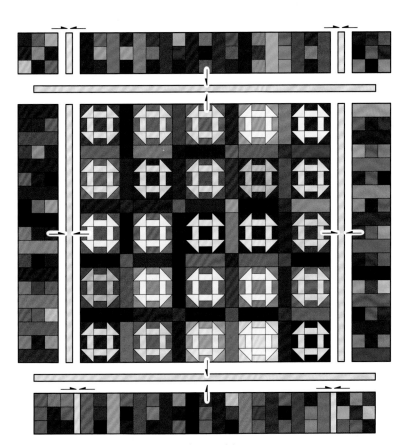

Quilt assembly

Sparkle

The chubby nature of the Wrench-style Churn Dash block lets the fabrics you choose stand on their own, yet the overall appeal remains scrappy. When I laid out the sashing strips in a stair-step pattern of two different colors, the quilt top sparkled, making it a quilt you can display year-round.

~ Jo

Materials

Yardage is based on 42" of usable fabric width after prewashing and removing selvages. Fat quarters are 18" × 21".

Approximately ½ yard *total* of assorted cream shirting prints for blocks

Approximately ¼ yard *total* of assorted red prints for blocks and cornerstones

Approximately ¼ yard *total* of assorted tan prints for blocks

Approximately ¼ yard *total* of assorted gray prints for blocks

1 fat quarter of tan print for sashing

1 fat quarter of gray check for sashing

1⅛ yards of red print for border and single-fold binding

1⅛ yards of fabric for backing

37" × 37" square of batting

Cutting

You'll need 25 Wrench blocks to complete the featured quilt. Cutting instructions are given for one block at a time for ease of having a block exchange; the number of pieces listed in parentheses provides the total amount needed to make 25 blocks.

For greater ease in piecing the blocks, keep the pieces for each block grouped together. The background pieces in each block are cut from the same shirting.

CUTTING FOR 1 WRENCH BLOCK

From *1* cream print, cut:
2 squares, 2½" × 2½" (total of 50)
1 square, 1½" × 1½" (total of 25)
1 strip, 1¼" × 6", from *lengthwise* grain (total of 25)

From *1* red, tan, or gray print, cut:
2 squares, 2½" × 2½" (total of 50)

From the *lengthwise* grain of a second red, tan, or gray print, cut:
1 strip, 1¼" × 6" (total of 25)

Continued on page 17

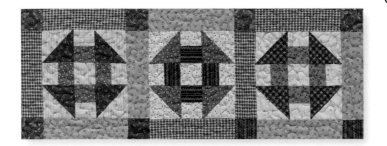

SWAP TALK

Whether you call them Churn Dashes, Wrenches, or even Hole in the Barn Door, these traditional quilt blocks are truly easy to make and offer another opportunity for you and your friends to play with fabrics. Here are a few ideas for just that!

❋ Make the side bars a different fabric from the corner half-square triangles. Sometimes I used two different shades of red, and sometimes I mixed in a charcoal or tan with red, but every block featured cream shirting print for the background—one shirting per block.

❋ Try to be specific with your color palette for a block exchange, so there are no surprises when it's time to swap. Colors have many different densities, so just saying red, tan, and gray might result in blocks that clash. Perhaps cut snippets of fabrics and send them around so everyone in the group is on the same page from the beginning.

❋ For the small half-square-triangle corners, your friends may like using foundation papers, which can make it easier to stitch accurately despite the small size. Here the units start with 2" squares and the finished units are just 1½" square.

❋ Share a photo of how you've pressed the back of your block. It's so helpful for quilt assembly and for quilting when all the blocks are pressed the same way. Consistent pressing gives you a consistent "ditch" for quilting.

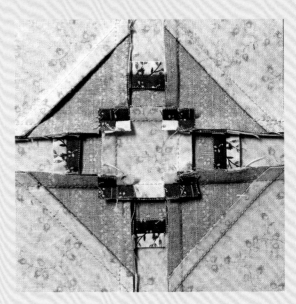

Continued from page 14

ADDITIONAL CUTTING TO COMPLETE THE QUILT

From the tan print for sashing, cut on the *lengthwise* grain:

10 strips, 1½" × 18"; crosscut into 30 rectangles, 1½" × 4½"

From the gray check for sashing, cut on the *lengthwise* grain:

10 strips, 1½" × 18"; crosscut into 30 rectangles, 1½" × 4½"

From assorted red prints, cut:

36 squares, 1½" × 1½"

From the red print for border and binding, cut on the *lengthwise* grain:

2 strips, 3½" × 26½"
2 strips, 3½" × 32½"

From the remainder of the red print, cut:

4 strips, 1⅛" × 42"

Piecing for 1 Wrench Block

Select a set of pieces cut for one block. For ease of explanation, we'll refer to the shirting prints as "light" and the red, tan, and gray prints as "dark." Use a scant ¼" seam throughout. After sewing each seam, press the seam allowances as indicated by the arrows.

1. Use a pencil and an acrylic ruler to draw a diagonal sewing line from corner to corner on the wrong side of each light 2½" square. Layer a marked square on top of a dark 2½" square right sides together. Stitch ¼" from each side of the drawn line. Cut apart on the drawn line to make two half-square-triangle units. Repeat with the remaining pair to

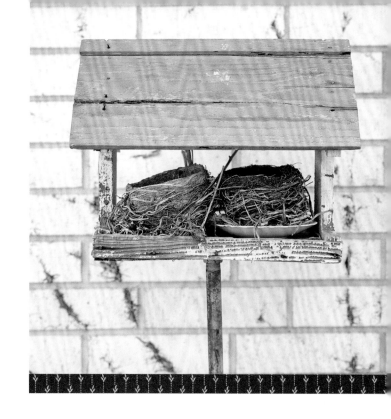

make a total of four half-square-triangle units. Square these units to measure 2" × 2".

Make 4 units,
2" x 2".

2. Place the dark and light 1¼" × 6" rectangles right sides together. Sew along one long edge. Press. Crosscut the strip set into four segments, 1½" × 2".

 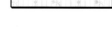

 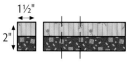

Cut 4 segments,
1½" x 2".

Finished quilt size: 32½" × 32½" • **Finished block size:** 4" × 4"

Designed and pieced by Jo Morton.
Machine quilted by Maggi Honeyman.

3. Arrange the half-square-triangle units, the 1½" × 2" pieced rectangles, and the light 1½" square in three rows, orienting the units as shown to make a Wrench block. Sew the units together in each row. Pin and then sew the rows together, matching the seam intersections.

Use "Jo's Clipping Trick" (page 120) at the seam intersections and press the seam allowances toward the rectangles and the clipped intersections open. The Wrench block should measure 4½" square, including the seam allowances.

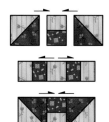

Wrench block,
4½" x 4½"

4. Repeat steps 1–3 to make a total of 25 Wrench blocks, mixing and matching the dark colors as desired.

Assembling the Quilt Top

1. Referring to the quilt photo on page 18 or the quilt assembly diagram on page 20, lay out the Wrench blocks in five rows of five blocks each, leaving room for the sashing strips and cornerstones. Place the gray sashing strips on the top and to the right of the top-left block. Add tan sashing strips on the bottom and to the left of the block. Now alternate the colors across the row horizontally as well as from row to row to create a stair-step effect. Place a red 1½" square at each intersection of the sashing strips.

2. Join five sashing strips and six red 1½" cornerstone squares, alternating the color of the sashing strips between the cornerstones as shown. Make three rows that start with a red cornerstone and gray sashing strip and make three rows that start with a red cornerstone and a tan sashing strip. All rows should measure 1½" × 26½".

Make 3 rows,
1½" x 26½".

Make 3 rows,
1½" x 26½".

3. Join five Wrench blocks and six sashing rectangles, alternating the gray and tan rectangles between the blocks. Make three rows that start with a gray sashing strip and

Quilt assembly

make two rows that start with a tan sashing strip. All rows should measure 4½" × 26½".

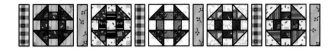

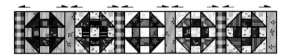

Make 3 rows,
4½" x 26½".

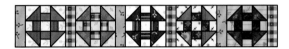

Make 2 rows,
4½" x 26½".

Sashing Placement

Keep an eye on your sashing strips and make sure that the colors at the left and top of each block match, with gray and tan alternating across each row for a stair-step effect.

4. Lay out the sashing rows and block rows in alternating positions as shown in the quilt assembly diagram, making sure that the rows are ordered correctly to create the stair-step effect in the sashing. Sew the rows together. The quilt top should measure 26½" square, including seam allowances.

5. Pin and then sew the red 3½" × 26½" border strips to the sides of quilt top. Pin and then sew the red 3½" × 32½" strips to the top and bottom of the quilt top. The quilt top should measure 32½" square.

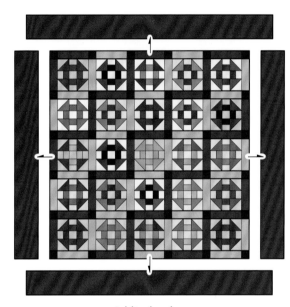

Adding borders

Completing the Quilt

Layer and baste the quilt top, batting, and backing. Quilt by hand or machine. The featured quilt was machine quilted with a small, allover meandering design. Referring to "Jo's Single-Fold Binding" on page 126, or substituting your favorite method, join the red print strips into one length and use it to bind the quilt.

Yesterday

Whether it's hanging over a cupboard door in my dining room, folded across the foot of the bed, hung on the wall, stacked with other scrappy beauties on a chair, or displayed in a vintage washing machine, Yesterday is one of my most cherished quilts. It reflects my love of Star blocks and Ohio Stars in particular.

~ Jo

SWAP TALK

Dig in to your scrap bin, cut from fabrics on your shelf, or visit your favorite quilt shop to achieve the look you want for your Ohio Star blocks and your Yesterday quilt. For my quilt, even though I used a red print for the setting squares, I repeated red in the background for three of the Star blocks, because the shades were slightly different. All the block backgrounds are darker than the stars, but some of the backgrounds are lighter compared to the rest of the blocks; the different values make the quilt shine. Antique quilts didn't follow any rules, and I like that.

This quilt of 30 blocks, each 6" square, is an ideal swap project to enter into with four friends. Each of you will make five sets of six blocks to exchange. It's the easiest way to get scrappy blocks; you only pick out five fabric sets, and the rest is magic.

Materials

Yardage is based on 42" of usable fabric width after prewashing and removing selvages.

Approximately 1 yard *total* of assorted cream shirting prints for blocks

Approximately 1¼ yard *total* of assorted medium and dark prints for blocks (collectively referred to as "dark")

1½ yard of red print for setting squares and triangles

1¾ yards of brown print for border

¼ yard of indigo print for single-fold binding

4 yards of fabric for backing

61" × 70" rectangle of batting

Cutting

You'll need 30 Ohio Star blocks. Cutting instructions are given for one block at a time; the number in parentheses provides the total amount needed for 30 blocks. For ease in piecing, keep the pieces for each block together as you cut. Of the 30 blocks, 29 use a shirting for the half-square triangles and the on-point center square, but one block also uses the striped shirting for the corner squares; can you find it?

CUTTING FOR 1 OHIO STAR BLOCK

From *1* cream print, cut:

2 squares, 3¼" × 3¼" (total of 60)
1 square, 2½" × 2½" (total of 30)

From *1* dark print, cut:

2 squares, 3¼" × 3¼" (total of 60)
4 squares, 2½" × 2½" (total of 120)

ADDITIONAL CUTTING TO COMPLETE THE QUILT

Cut all pieces across the width of the fabric in the order given unless otherwise noted.

From the red print, cut:

20 squares, 6½" × 6½"
5 squares, 10½" × 10½"; cut each square into quarters diagonally to yield 20 side setting triangles (you will have 2 triangles left over)*
2 squares, 6" × 6"; cut each square in half diagonally to yield 4 corner triangles

From the brown print, cut on the *lengthwise* grain:

2 strips, 6½" × 51½"
2 strips, 6½" × 55"

From the indigo print, cut:

7 strips, 1⅛" × 42"

*The setting triangles are cut slightly oversized so you can square up the quilt top before adding the border.

Piecing for 1 Ohio Star Block

Use a scant ¼" seam allowance throughout (a thread or two less than a full ¼"). After sewing each seam, press the seam allowances as indicated by the arrows.

1. Select a set of pieces cut for one block. Using a pencil and an acrylic ruler, draw a diagonal line from corner to corner on the wrong side of each cream 3¼" square. Layer a marked square on top of a dark 3¼" square right sides together. Stitch a scant ¼" from each side of the drawn line. Cut apart on the drawn line to make two half-square-triangle units; press. Repeat with the remaining pair to make a second half-square triangle for a total of four matching half-square-triangle units.

Make 4 units,
2⅞" × 2⅞".

Finished quilt size: 55" × 63½" • **Finished block size:** 6" × 6"

Designed and pieced by Jo Morton.
Machine quilted by Maggi Honeyman.

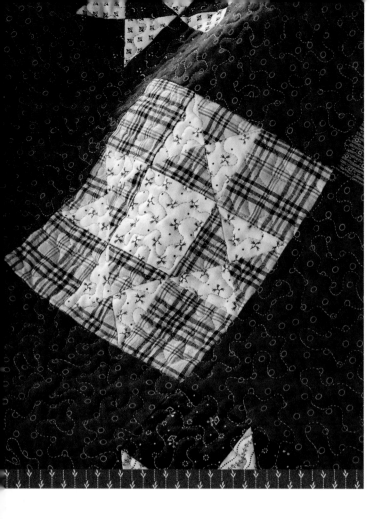

3. Arrange the hourglass units, the cream 2½" square, and the four dark 2½" squares in three rows. Make sure the hourglass units form a star (that is, the dark fabric of each one touches the center light square) before you join the units. Sew the units together in rows.

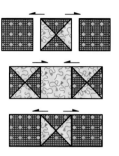

4. Pin and then sew the rows together, matching seam intersections. Use the clipping trick at the seam intersections and press. The Ohio Star block should measure 6½" square, including seam allowances.

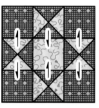

Ohio Star block,
6½" x 6½"

5. Repeat steps 1–4 to make a total of 30 Ohio Star blocks.

2. Layer two half-square-triangle units, right sides together and seams abutted, and with the light fabric facing the dark fabric. Draw a diagonal line that is perpendicular to the seam. Sew a scant ¼" from each side of the drawn line. Cut the units apart on the drawn line and square up to make two hourglass units that measure 2½" × 2½". Use "Jo's Clipping Trick" (page 120) at the seam intersection, pressing the seam allowances toward the dark fabric. Make a total of four matching hourglass units.

Make 4 units,
2½" x 2½".

Fabric Favorites

If you've been saving a special fabric, the best place to store it is in a quilt!

Assembling the Quilt Top

1. Arrange the blocks, the red 6½" squares, and the red setting triangles in diagonal rows as shown. Sew the pieces together into rows; press. Join the rows, matching the seam intersections. Add the corner triangles last. Use my clipping trick at all seam intersections to press the allowances toward the setting squares and triangles.

2. Trim and square up the quilt top to measure 43" × 51½", including seam allowances, making sure to leave a ¼" seam allowance beyond all points.

3. Pin and sew the brown 6½" × 51½" border strips to opposite sides of the quilt. Press the seam allowances toward the border. Pin and sew the brown 6½" × 55" border strips to the top and bottom of the quilt. Press the seam allowances toward the border. The quilt top should measure 55" × 63½".

Completing the Quilt

Layer and baste the quilt top, batting, and backing. Quilt the layers. The featured quilt was machine quilted with an allover meandering design. Referring to "Jo's Single-Fold Binding" on page 126, or substituting your own method, use the indigo strips to bind the quilt.

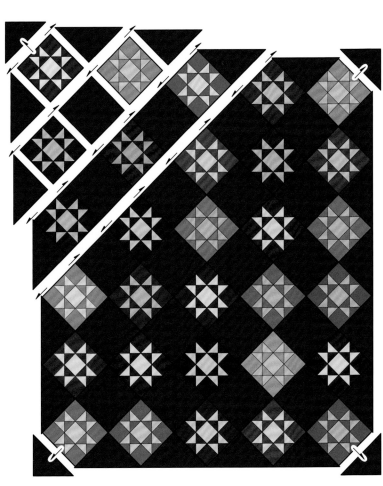

Quilt assembly

Star Spangled

What could possibly be better than a star block? A whole bundle of them! Surround your stitched stars with simple squares and scrappy four patches for extra sizzle and sparkle, and this patchwork quilt will be sure to deliver the drama.

~ Kim

SWAP TALK

For the Ohio Star block variation featured in this exchange, I suggest pairing a richly hued print with a subtle black print to form the framed star design and define it well. Fabric requirements for the scrappy block triangles and checkerboard sashing rows are outlined in the materials list, but keep in mind that this is an ideal project for taking a "more the merrier" approach and raiding your stash to incorporate a huge variety of prints. If desired for this exchange, a 2½" × 21" strip of your chosen black print can be swapped in with each block to produce a scrappy pieced binding, or you can opt for a single complementary black print—the choice is yours!

Materials

Yardage is based on 42" of usable fabric width after prewashing and removing selvages. Fat eighths are 9" × 21", chubby sixteenths are 9" × 10½", and charm squares are 5" × 5".

9 fat eighths of assorted black prints for Ohio Star blocks and binding*

9 fat eighths of assorted medium and dark prints (collectively referred to as "dark") for blocks

9 fat eighths of assorted cream prints for blocks

36 charm squares of assorted dark prints for blocks (4 charm squares per block), or equivalent scraps from multiple assorted prints

18 chubby sixteenths of assorted prints for checkerboard sashing

3 yards of fabric for backing

51" × 51" square of batting

*If you prefer to use a single print for binding, you'll need an additional ½ yard of fabric for binding.

Cutting

You'll need nine Ohio Star Variation blocks to complete the featured quilt. Cutting instructions are given for one block at a time; the number of pieces listed in parentheses provides the total amount needed to make nine blocks. For greater ease in piecing the blocks, keep the pieces for each block grouped together as you cut them.

CUTTING FOR 1 OHIO STAR VARIATION BLOCK

From *1* black print, cut:
1 strip, 5¼" × 21"; from this strip, cut:
   2 squares, 5¼" × 5¼" (combined total of 18);
     cut each square in half diagonally *twice* to
     yield 4 triangles (8 per block; combined
     total of 72)
   1 square, 4½" × 4½" (combined total of 9)
1 binding strip, 2½" × 21" (combined total of
   9). (For Kim's Chubby Binding method
   provided on page 127, reduce the strip width
   to 2".) See "Swap Talk" on page 28.

From *1* dark print, cut:
1 strip, 5¼" × 21"; from this strip, cut:
   1 square, 5¼" × 5¼" (combined total of 9); cut
     the square in half diagonally *twice* to yield
     4 triangles (combined total of 36)
   2 squares, 3⅞" × 3⅞" (combined total of 18);
     cut each square in half diagonally *once* to
     yield 2 triangles (4 per block; combined
     total of 36)

From *1* cream print, cut:
1 strip, 5¼" × 21"; from this strip, cut:
   1 square, 5¼" × 5¼" (total of 9); cut the
     square in half diagonally *twice* to yield
     4 triangles (combined total of 36)
   2 squares, 3⅞" × 3⅞" (total of 18); cut each
     square in half diagonally *once* to yield
     2 triangles (4 per block; combined total
     of 36)
   2 squares, 1⅞" × 1⅞" (total of 18); cut each
     square in half diagonally *once* to yield
     2 triangles (4 per block; combined total
     of 36)
   4 squares, 1½" × 1½" (combined total of 36)
1 strip, 1⅞" × 21"; crosscut into 10 squares,
   1⅞" × 1⅞" (12 total per block when combined
   with previously cut 1⅞" squares; combined
   total of 108). Cut each square in half
   diagonally *once* to yield 2 triangles (24 per
   block; combined total of 216).

From *each of 4* dark print charm squares (or equivalent scraps from multiple prints), cut:
3 squares, 1⅞" × 1⅞" (total of 12); cut each square
   in half diagonally *once* to yield 2 triangles
   (24 per block; combined total of 216)

ADDITIONAL CUTTING

Cut all pieces across the width of the fabric in the order given unless otherwise noted.

From the 18 assorted print chubby sixteenths, cut a *combined total* of:
150 squares, 2½" × 2½"
70 squares, 1½" × 1½"

From the coordinating black print (if you've opted not to exchange strips for a scrappy binding), cut:
5 strips, 2½" × 42" (For Kim's Chubby Binding
   method provided on page 127, reduce the
   strip width to 2".)

Finished quilt size: 44½" × 44½" • **Finished block size:** 12" × 12"

Designed by Kim Diehl. Pieced by Julia Wareing and Kim Diehl.
Machine quilted by Rebecca Silbaugh.

four pieced large half-square-triangle units measuring 3½" square, including the seam allowances.

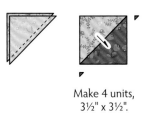

Make 4 units,
3½" x 3½".

3. Join, press, and trim the cream and dark 1⅞" triangles as in step 2 to make a total of 24 pieced half-square-triangle units measuring 1½" square, including the seam allowances.

Make 24 units,
1½" x 1½".

Piecing for 1 Ohio Star Variation Block

The steps that follow will make one block. Repeat these steps to make nine blocks. Sew all pieces with right sides together using a ¼" seam allowance unless otherwise noted. Press the seam allowances as indicated by the arrows or as otherwise specified.

1. Select a set of pieces cut for one Ohio Star Variation block. Lay out two black 5¼" triangles, one dark 5¼" triangle, and one cream 5¼" triangle as shown. Join the triangles in each diagonal row. Press. Trim away the dog-ear points. Join the rows. Press. Trim away the dog-ear points. Repeat to make a total of four pieced hourglass units measuring 4½" square, including the seam allowances.

4. Referring to the illustration and choosing prints randomly, lay out three small half-square-triangle units. Join and press. Repeat to make a total of four half-square-triangle rows and four mirror-image rows measuring 1½" × 3½", including the seam allowances.

Make 4 each,
1½" x 3½".

5. Lay out one half-square-triangle unit from step 2, one half-square-triangle row, one mirror-image row, and one cream 1½" square in two horizontal rows. Join the pieces in each row. Press. Join the rows. Press. Repeat for a total of four block corner units measuring 4½" square, including the seam allowances.

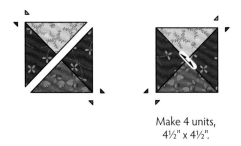

Make 4 units,
4½" x 4½".

2. Join a cream and a dark 3⅞" triangle along the long diagonal edges. Press. Trim away the dog-ear points. Repeat to make a total of

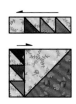

Make 4 units,
4½" x 4½".

6. Lay out four hourglass units, four block corner units, and one black 4½" square in three horizontal rows. Join the pieces in each row. Press. Join the rows. Press to complete an Ohio Star Variation block that measures 12½" square, including seam allowances.

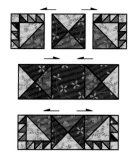
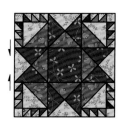

Ohio Star Variation block, 12½" x 12½"

7. Repeat steps 1–6 to make a total of nine Ohio Star Variation blocks.

Piecing the Checkerboard Sashing

1. Choosing the prints randomly, lay out four assorted print 1½" squares in two rows. Join the squares in each row. Press. Join the rows. Press. Repeat to make a total of 16 four-patch units measuring 2½" square, including the seam allowances. (You'll have six leftover 1½" squares.)

Make 16 units, 2½" x 2½".

2. Choosing randomly, join six assorted 2½" squares end to end. Press. Repeat for a total of 24 checkerboard sashing strips measuring 2½" × 12½", including the seam allowances. (You'll have six leftover 2½" squares.)

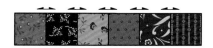

Make 24 units, 2½" x 12½".

Piecing the Quilt Top

1. Lay out four four-patch units and three checkerboard sashing strips in alternating positions. Join the pieces. Press. Repeat to make a total of four sashing rows measuring 2½" × 44½", including the seam allowances.

Make 4 rows, 2½" x 44½".

2. Lay out four checkerboard sashing strips and three Ohio Star Variation blocks in alternating positions. Join the pieces. Press the seam allowances toward the checkerboard strips. Repeat to make a total of three block rows measuring 12½" × 44½", including the seam allowances.

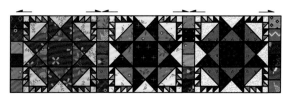

Make 3 rows, 12½" x 44½".

3. Referring to the photo on page 31, lay out the four pieced checkerboard sashing rows and the three pieced block rows in alternating positions. Join the rows. Press.

Completing the Quilt

Layer and baste the quilt top, batting, and backing. Quilt the layers. The featured quilt was machine quilted with parallel straight lines in the stars, and curved lines arching from one corner of each square in the border and sashing to the next. Referring to "Kim's Chubby Binding" on page 127, or substituting your own favorite method, use the binding strips to bind the quilt.

Ohio Star Mini-Quilt

Finished quilt size: 8½" × 8½"

The traditional Ohio Star block is versatile, fun to stitch, and a perfect starting point for building this quick and easy mini-quilt. Use the pictured project as a guide when choosing your print colors (or substitute your own favorite color scheme), raid your stash of fabrics, and let the stitching begin!

Materials and Cutting

Medium blue print for star center:
1 square, 2½" × 2½"

Light blue print for star points:
2 squares, 3¼" × 3¼"; cut each square in half diagonally *twice* to yield 4 triangles (total of 8)

Cream print for star background:
2 squares, 3¼" × 3¼"; cut each square in half diagonally *twice* to yield 4 triangles (total of 8)
4 squares, 1½" × 1½"

Brown check or print for block setting:
8 squares, 1½" × 1½"
4 rectangles, 1½" × 2½"

Tan print for block setting:
8 squares, 1½" × 1½"
2 squares, 2⅞" × 2⅞"; cut each square in half diagonally *once* to yield 2 triangles (total of 4)

Dark brown print for block corners:
2 squares, 2⅞" × 2⅞"; cut each square in half diagonally *once* to yield 2 triangles (total of 4)

Dark brown print for binding:
1 strip, 2½" × 44" (For Kim's Chubby Binding method provided on page 127, reduce the strip width to 2".)

Backing:
1 square, 12" × 12"

Batting:
1 square, 15" × 15"

Piecing the Quilt Top

1. Lay out two cream and two light blue triangles. Join the triangles along their short edges as shown. Press. Trim away the dog-ear points. Join the resulting pieced triangles. Press. Trim away the dog-ear points. Repeat to make a total of four hourglass units measuring 2½" square, including the seam allowances.

Make 4 units,
2½" x 2½".

2. Join the tan and brown check 1½" squares to make a total of eight pieced rectangles measuring 1½" × 2½", including the seam allowances. Press.

Make 8 units,
1½" x 2½".

3. Join a cream 1½" square to the brown end of four of the pieced rectangles to make units measuring 1½" × 3½", including the seam allowances. Press.

Make 4 units,
1½" x 3½".

4. Join a tan and dark brown 2⅞" triangle along the long diagonal edges. Press. Trim away the dog-ear points. Repeat to make a total of four half-square-triangle units measuring 2½" square, including the seam allowances.

5. Join a step 2 pieced rectangle to a tan and brown half-square-triangle unit. Press.

Repeat to make a total of four units measuring 2½" × 3½", including the seam allowances.

Make 4 units,
2½" x 3½".

6. Join a step 3 unit to a step 5 unit as shown. Press. Repeat to make a total of four corner units measuring 3½" square, including the seam allowances.

Make 4 units,
3½" x 3½".

7. Join a brown check 1½" × 2½" rectangle to a cream edge of an hourglass unit from step 1. Press the seam allowances toward the brown rectangle. Repeat to make a total of four units measuring 2½" × 3½", including the seam allowances.

8. Lay out the units and medium blue square as shown. Join the pieces in each horizontal row. Press. Then join the rows; press.

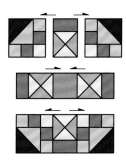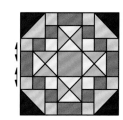

Quilt assembly

9. Layer and baste the quilt top, batting, and backing. Quilt the layers as desired. Use the dark brown binding strip to bind the quilt.

Field of Greens

Because of their charm, Hearth and Home blocks have been a perennial favorite of generations of quiltmakers. Wonderful all on their own, these blocks become even better when signed by their makers, because they'll transform your quilt into a priceless keepsake of special memories and friends.

~ Kim

SWAP TALK

Unbleached muslin is an ideal choice for the background of this project because it lends a soft, vintage feel and enables the stitched quilting design to really shine. For my quilt, I chose shades of mossy green for the patchwork, but any color that makes you happy will work perfectly—rich indigo blues, vibrant hues of crimson, or even sunny shades of cheddar. To give your finished quilt a beautifully cohesive look, cut a handful of extra rectangles and squares from each print to exchange with the blocks for the remaining border patchwork.

Materials

Yardage is based on 42" of usable fabric width after prewashing and removing selvages. Charm squares are 5" × 5".

36 squares, 10" × 10", of assorted medium and dark green prints for blocks and middle and outer pieced borders

1⅞ yards of unbleached muslin for patchwork

¾ yard of medium green print for pieced sashing and outer pieced border

⅔ yard of dark green print for inner border and binding

4 charm squares of assorted green prints for middle pieced border

3⅓ yards of fabric for backing

60" × 60" square of batting

Cutting

You'll need 36 Hearth and Home blocks to complete the center of the featured quilt (the blocks for the outer border corners will be pieced separately). Cutting instructions are given for one block at a time; the number of pieces listed in parentheses provides the total amount needed to make 36 blocks. For greater ease in piecing the blocks, keep the pieces for each block grouped together as you cut them.

CUTTING FOR 1 HEARTH AND HOME BLOCK

From *1* green 10" square, cut:

1 strip, 1⅞" × 10"; crosscut each strip into:
    4 squares, 1⅞" × 1⅞" (combined total of 144). Cut each square in half diagonally *once* to yield 2 triangles (8 total per block; combined total of 288).
    1 square, 1½" × 1½" (combined total of 36)*
5 strips, 1½" × 10"; crosscut *each* strip into:
    1 rectangle, 1½" × 5½" (5 total; combined total of 180)*
    2 squares, 1½" × 1½" (10 total; combined total of 360—396 in all, including the previously cut 1½" squares)*

From the unbleached muslin, cut:

6 squares, 1½" × 1½" (combined total of 216)
1 rectangle, 1½" × 3½" (combined total of 36)
4 squares, 1⅞" × 1⅞" (combined total of 144); cut each square in half diagonally *once* to yield 2 triangles (8 total per block; combined total of 288)

From each of the 36 green prints, set aside 5 rectangles, 1½" × 5½", and 3 squares, 1½" × 1½". These pieces won't be used for the blocks but could be swapped as part of a block exchange and used in the pieced border.

ADDITIONAL CUTTING TO COMPLETE THE QUILT

Cut all pieces across the width of the fabric in the order given unless otherwise noted.

From the medium green print, cut:

12 strips, 1½" × 42"; crosscut *4 strips* into 104 squares, 1½" × 1½". Reserve the remaining strips for the strip sets.
3 strips, 1⅞" × 42"; crosscut into 52 squares, 1⅞" × 1⅞". Cut each square in half diagonally *once* to yield 2 triangles (total of 104).

From the unbleached muslin, cut:

13 strips, 1½" × 42"; crosscut *8 strips* into 42 squares, 1½" × 1½", and 65 rectangles, 1½" × 3½". Reserve the remaining strips for the strip sets.
3 strips, 1⅞" × 42"; crosscut into 56 squares, 1⅞" × 1⅞". Cut each square in half diagonally *once* to yield 2 triangles (total of 112).

From the dark green print, cut:

4 strips, 1½" × 42"; crosscut into 2 strips, 1½" × 39½", and 2 strips, 1½" × 41½"
6 binding strips, 2½" × 42" (For Kim's Chubby Binding method on page 127, reduce the strip width to 2".)

From *each* charm square of assorted green print, cut:

1 square, 1⅞" × 1⅞"; cut each square in half diagonally *once* to yield 2 triangles (combined total of 8)
1 square, 1½" × 1½" (combined total of 4)

Finished quilt size: 53½" × 53½" • **Finished block size:** 5" × 5"

Designed and pieced by Kim Diehl.
Machine quilted by Rebecca Silbaugh.

Piecing for 1 Hearth and Home Block

The steps that follow will make one block. Repeat these steps to make 36 blocks. Sew all pieces with right sides together using a ¼" seam allowance unless otherwise noted. Press the seam allowances as indicated by the arrows or as otherwise specified.

1. Select a set of green pieces cut for one patchwork block (eight green 1⅞" triangles and eight matching green 1½" squares). Add eight muslin 1⅞" triangles, six muslin 1½" squares, and one muslin 1½" × 3½" rectangle.

2. Join a green and a muslin 1⅞" triangle along the long diagonal edges. Press. Trim away the dog-ear points. Repeat to make a total of eight half-square-triangle units measuring 1½" square, including the seam allowances.

Make 8 units,
1½" x 1½".

3. Join half-square-triangle units to opposite sides of a green 1½" square as shown. Press. Repeat to make a total of four triangle units measuring 1½" × 3½", including the seam allowances.

Make 4 units,
1½" x 3½".

4. Join green 1½" squares to opposite sides of a muslin 1½" square. Press. Repeat to make a total of two units measuring 1½" × 3½", including the seam allowances.

Make 2 units,
1½" x 3½".

5. Sew the units from step 4 to opposite sides of a muslin 1½" × 3½" rectangle. Press. The block center unit should measure 3½" square, including the seam allowances.

Make 1 unit,
3½" x 3½".

6. Join step 3 triangle units to opposite sides of the pieced center block unit. Press.

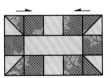

Make 1 unit,
3½" x 5½".

7. Join a muslin 1½" square to each end of the remaining step 3 pieced triangle units. Press. Join these pieced units to the remaining sides of the center block unit. Press. The pieced Hearth and Home block should measure 5½" square, including the seam allowances.

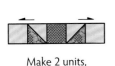

Make 2 units,
1½" x 5½".

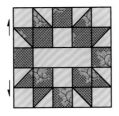

Hearth and Home block,
5½" x 5½".

8. Repeat steps 1–7 to make a total of 36 Hearth and Home blocks.

Signature Guidelines

If you've opted to exchange signed blocks as a special remembrance of this project, I suggest establishing a handful of simple guidelines to ensure that no single signed block becomes a "bulls-eye." As a group, decide upon a preferred ink color and choose a type of pen that will be readily available to all participants. For instance, Micron Pigma markers can be found in many quilt shops or purchased online, in a wide range of colors (black or brown is a good choice for many color schemes), and there are several tip sizes to choose from.

To stabilize the signature area of each block for signing, cut a rectangle of freezer paper to fit the space and use a hot, dry iron to fuse it to the *wrong* side of the fabric from the back of the block. After the block has been signed, peel away the freezer paper. Easy!

Piecing the Sashing Units

1. Join a green 1½" × 42" strip to each long side of a muslin 1½" × 42" strip. Press. Repeat to make a total of four pieced strip sets. Crosscut the strip sets to make 12 long strip-set units, 3½" × 8½", and 12 short strip-set units, 3½" × 4½".

Make 4 strip sets,
3½" x 42".

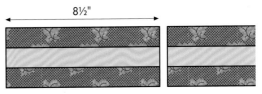

Cut 12 long units, 3½" x 8½".

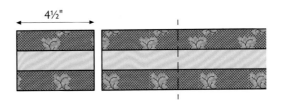

Cut 12 short units, 3½" x 4½".

2. Using the medium green and muslin 1⅞" triangles, follow step 2 of "Piecing for 1 Hearth and Home Block" on page 40 to make 104 medium green 1½" half-square-triangle units.

Make 104 units,
1½" x 1½".

3. Using the medium green 1½" squares and the 104 half-square-triangle units, repeat step 3 of "Piecing for 1 Hearth and Home Block" on page 40 to make 52 triangle units.

Make 52 units,
1½" x 3½".

4. Join a triangle unit to a short strip unit as shown. Press. Repeat to make a total of 12 short sashing units measuring 3½" × 5½", including the seam allowances.

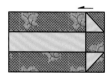

Make 12 short units,
3½" x 5½".

5. Join a pieced triangle unit to each short end of a long strip unit. Press. Repeat to make a total of 12 long sashing units measuring 3½" × 10½", including the seam allowances. Reserve the remaining medium green triangle units for the outer border.

Make 12 long units,
3½" x 10½".

6. Using 52 medium green 1½" squares, 26 muslin 1½" squares, and 13 muslin 1½" × 3½" rectangles, repeat steps 4 and 5 of "Piecing for 1 Hearth and Home Block" on page 40 to make 13 medium green center block units.

Make 13 units,
3½" x 3½".

Piecing the Quilt Center

1. Lay out and join six Hearth and Home blocks and three short sashing units as shown to make row A. Press. Repeat to make a total of two A rows measuring 5½" × 39½", including the seam allowances.

Make 2 A rows, 5½" x 39½".

Strategic Color Placement

When laying out my patchwork blocks for quilt-top assembly, I've learned that placing those with lighter or more subdued colors in the corner positions can weaken the design, because the shape of the corner can appear to fade away. Instead, I consistently place blocks with stronger hues in the corner positions to anchor the patchwork and keep the shape of each corner well defined. Keep this tip in mind as you lay out and piece the A rows (and also the end positions of the piano key borders on page 45), because this approach will result in a finished project with a thoughtful, balanced, and polished look.

2. Lay out and join two short sashing units, three medium green center block units, and two long sashing units as shown to make row B. Press. Repeat to make a total of three B rows measuring 3½" × 39½", including the seam allowances. Reserve the remaining medium green center block units for use in the border.

Make 3 B rows, 3½" x 39½".

3. Join two pieced Hearth and Home blocks as shown. Press. Repeat to make a total of 12 block pairs.

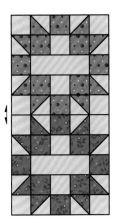

Make 12 block pairs.

4. Lay out and join six block pairs and three long sashing units as shown. Press. Repeat to make a total of two C rows measuring 10½" × 39½", including the seam allowances.

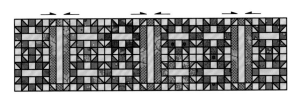

Make 2 C rows, 10½" x 39½".

5. Referring to the pictured quilt on page 39, lay out the pieced A, B, and C rows in this order: A, B, C, B, C, B, A. Join the rows. Press the seam allowances toward the B rows. The quilt center should measure 39½" square, including the seam allowances.

Adding the Inner Border

1. Join a dark green 1½" × 39½" strip to the right and left sides of the quilt center. Press the seam allowance toward the dark green strips.

2. Join the dark green 1½" × 41½" strips to the remaining sides of the quilt center. Press the seam allowances toward the green strips. The quilt top should now measure 41½" square, including the seam allowances.

Piecing and Adding the Middle Border

1. Use a pencil and an acrylic ruler to draw a diagonal sewing line from corner to corner on the wrong side of 104 assorted green print 1½" squares.

2. Layer a prepared green 1½" square onto each short end of a muslin 1½" × 3½" rectangle as shown. Stitch the squares along the drawn lines. Fold the resulting inner triangles open, aligning the corners with the corners of the muslin rectangle. Press. Trim away the layers beneath the top triangles, leaving ¼" seam allowances. Repeat to make a total of 52 pieced flying-geese-variation units measuring 1½" × 3½", including the seam allowances. (You'll have four leftover squares.)

Make 52 units,
1½" x 3½".

3. Using the muslin and assorted green print 1⅞" triangles, repeat step 3 of "Piecing for 1 Hearth and Home Block" on page 40 to make eight half-square-triangle units.

4. Using the quilt assembly diagram on page 45 as a guide, join 13 flying-geese-variation units end to end. Press the seam allowances open. Repeat to make a total of four pieced strips measuring 1½" × 39½", including the seam allowances.

5. Join a half-square-triangle unit from step 3 to each end of the step 4 pieced strips. Press the seam allowances open. Join two of these pieced border strips to the right and left sides of the quilt top. Press the seam allowances toward the dark green border. Join a green print 1½" square to each end of the remaining pieced strips. Press the seam allowances toward the green squares. Join these strips to the top and bottom edges of the quilt top. Press the seam allowances toward the green border. The quilt top should now measure 43½" square, including the seam allowances.

Piecing and Adding the Outer Border

1. Join 43 assorted green 1½" × 5½" rectangles side by side. (Because there will be little stretch to the completed unit after the rectangles have been joined, I suggest using a very slightly scant ¼" seam allowance. This approach will compensate for the lack of stretch when the outer-border units are joined to the quilt center; any excess strip length can be adjusted by trimming the unit ends or making slight adjustments to the sewn seams of one or two rectangles.) Press the seam allowances to one side (the direction won't matter!). Repeat to make a total of four piano-key border strips measuring 5½" × 43½", including the seam allowances. (You'll have eight leftover rectangles.)

2. Using the reserved medium green triangle units, the reserved medium green center block units, and 16 muslin 1½" squares,

follow steps 6 and 7 of "Piecing for 1 Hearth and Home Block" on page 40 to make four corner blocks for the outer border.

3. Join a step 1 piano-key border strip to the right and left sides of the quilt top. Press the seam allowances toward the pieced border. Join a block from step 2 to each end of the remaining piano-key border strips. Press the seam allowances toward the border strip. Join these strips to the top and bottom edges of the quilt top. Press the seam allowances toward the outer border.

Completing the Quilt

Layer and baste the quilt top, batting, and backing. Quilt the layers. The featured quilt was machine quilted with a Baptist Fan design in the quilt center. The inner border was crosshatched, the middle border was stitched with repeating curved lines to form a swag design, and the outer border was stitched with a curling feather. Referring to "Kim's Chubby Binding" method on page 127, or substituting your own favorite method, use the binding strips to bind the quilt.

Quilt assembly

Harvest Home

Small blocks can add up to make a big impact! Here, in a three-color combo of tan, indigo, and cream, this little quilt makes an inviting topper for a harvest table as it establishes a gorgeous foundation for a display of redware, yellowware, or Polish pottery. Position Harvest Home on point on your dining surface for an added decorative touch.

~ Jo

Materials

Yardage is based on 42" of usable fabric width after prewashing and removing selvages.

Approximately ½ yard *total* of 9 assorted indigo prints for blocks

Approximately ½ yard *total* of 9 assorted cream shirting prints for blocks

⅝ yard of tan print for setting squares and triangles

¼ yard of indigo print for single-fold binding

1 yard of fabric for backing

31" × 31" square of batting

Cutting

You'll need nine Hearth and Home blocks to complete the featured table topper. Cutting is given for one block at a time for ease of having a block exchange; the number of pieces listed in parentheses provides the total amount needed to make nine blocks. For greater ease in piecing the blocks, keep the pieces for each block grouped together as you cut them.

CUTTING FOR 1 HEARTH AND HOME BLOCK

From *1 indigo print*, cut:
4 squares, 2¼" × 2¼" (total of 36)
8 squares, 1¾" × 1¾" (total of 72)

From *1 cream print*, cut:
1 rectangle, 1¾" × 4¼" (total of 9)
4 squares, 2¼" × 2¼" (total of 36)
6 squares, 1¾" × 1¾" (total of 54)

SWAP TALK

Isn't it funny how we get used to some blocks and use them over and over? This block is a new design for me, and I'm happy to add it to my list of favorites. It offers a bonus feature: the center bar can be a solid or near-solid fabric if you wish to make friendship blocks with signatures. It wouldn't be hard to convince your stitch group to get on board with this. In future years, you'll look at your quilt with lovely memories of your stitch friends.

❈ While my quilt has nine blocks, let's say you've decided to make a quilt with a setting that needs 16 blocks. Find three friends and you can each make four sets of four blocks to exchange. It's a quick and easy way to make a quilt with lots of different coordinating fabrics.

❈ Speaking of fabrics, once you and your swap sisters have started on a color scheme, try picking through the fat quarter trays at quilt shops, and then search the shelves. Even better, take your sewing buddies to the quilt shop (road trip ahead), and select the fabrics together. I usually take home at least a few fat quarters to add to my scrappy fabric collection. Sometimes when I want 2 yards of a fabric, I'll buy 2½ yards and cut off a half yard for the shelf, and then the 2-yard piece goes in a stack for setting or borders.

ADDITIONAL CUTTING TO COMPLETE THE QUILT

Cut all pieces across the width of the fabric in the order given unless otherwise noted.

From the tan print, cut:
2 squares, 10¾" × 10¾"; cut each square into quarters diagonally to yield 8 side setting triangles

6 squares, 6¾" × 6¾"; cut *2* of the squares in half diagonally to yield 4 corner triangles

From the binding fabric, cut:
3 strips, 1⅛" × 42"

Piecing for 1 Hearth and Home Block

Use a scant ¼" seam throughout. After sewing each seam, press the seam allowances as indicated by the arrows.

1. Select a set of pieces cut for one block. Use a pencil and an acrylic ruler to draw a diagonal sewing line from corner to corner on the wrong side of each cream 2¼" square. Layer a marked cream square on top of an indigo 2¼" square with right sides together. Stitch the pair of layered squares together ¼" from each side of the drawn line. Cut apart on the drawn line to make two half-square-triangle units. Repeat with the remaining pairs to make a total of eight half-square-triangle units. Square these units to measure 1¾" × 1¾".

Make 8 units,
1¾" x 1¾".

Finished quilt size: 27" × 27" • **Finished block size:** 6¼" × 6¼"

Designed and pieced by Jo Morton.
Machine quilted by Maggi Honeyman.

2. Lay out the half-square-triangle units, the eight indigo 1¾" squares, the six cream 1¾" squares, and the cream 1¾" × 4¼" rectangle, making sure to orient the half-square triangles as shown. Join the pieces in each row.

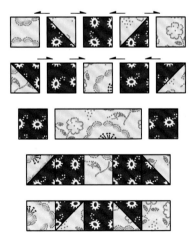

3. Pin and then sew the rows together, matching the seam intersections. Refer to "Jo's Clipping Trick" (page 120) to clip the seam intersections. Press the clipped intersections open and the seam allowances toward the dark squares. The block should measure 6¾" square, including seam allowances.

Hearth and Home block,
6¾" x 6¾"

4. Repeat step 1–3 to make a total of nine Hearth and Home blocks.

Assembling the Quilt Top

1. Referring to the quilt assembly diagram, arrange the blocks, the tan 6¾" squares, and the tan side setting triangles into diagonal rows. Sew the pieces in each row together; press. Pin and then sew the rows, matching the seam intersections. Clip the intersections. Press the clipped intersections open and the seam allowances toward the setting fabric. Add the tan corner triangles last and press.

2. Carefully trim away the excess fabric, leaving a ¼" seam allowance beyond the corners of the blocks. The finished quilt top should measure 27" square.

Completing the Quilt

Layer and baste the quilt top, batting, and backing. Quilt by hand or machine. The featured quilt was machine quilted with an allover meandering design. Referring to "Jo's Single-Fold Binding" technique on page 126, or substituting your own method, use the binding strips to bind the quilt.

Why No Borders?

I usually have a reason for the quilts I make. Since I had a purpose in mind for this table topper, I felt a border would be heavy and take away from the pottery items I wanted to display.

Not every quilt needs to be the star in the room; sometimes the supporting cast is equally important. Of course, if you have a "larger" purpose in mind for your Harvest Home quilt, by all means, add borders!

Quilt assembly

Gaggle of Geese

It's fun sometimes to go big and bold when quilting, but designs that blend a limited palette in subtle prints are the ones that comfortably nestle into our surroundings, looking as if they've always been there. Two different half-square-triangle blocks are all you need to make this warm yet structured design, which gives the illusion of having been pieced on point.

~ Jo

Materials

Yardage is based on 42" of usable fabric width after prewashing and removing selvages.

Approximately 1½ yards *total* of cream shirting prints for blocks

Approximately 1 yard *total* of assorted red prints for blocks

Approximately ½ yard *total* of assorted brown prints for blocks

¼ yard of red print for binding

1¼ yards of fabric for backing

44" × 44" square of batting

Cutting

You'll need 36 Flock of Geese blocks to complete the featured quilt. Cutting is given for one block at a time for ease of having a block exchange; the number of pieces listed in parentheses provides the total amount needed to make 36 blocks. (See "Swap Talk" on page 54.) *For greater ease in piecing the blocks, keep the pieces for each block grouped together. Try to avoid repeating identical print placement within one block.*

CUTTING FOR 1 FLOCK OF GEESE BLOCK

From *1* cream print, cut:
1 square, 5½" × 5½" (total of 36)
1 square, 4" × 4" (total of 36)

From *1* red print, cut:
1 square, 5½" × 5½" (total of 36)

From *1* brown print, cut:
1 square, 4" × 4" (total of 36)

ADDITIONAL CUTTING TO COMPLETE THE QUILT

Cut all pieces across the width of the fabric in the order given unless otherwise noted.

From the binding fabric, cut:
4 strips, 1⅛" × 42"

SWAP TALK

To make this quilt as a block exchange among friends, start by choosing a color scheme you all agree on. In my quilt the larger triangles are all brown and cream, and the smaller ones are red and cream. Choose a three-color scheme like this, or decide that totally scrappy is your preference. Either way, it's good to pick a common background color, such as the creams used here, to make the "geese" stand out.

The quilt is made with 6" blocks—36 of them to be exact—so if you team with five friends, each of you can make six sets of six blocks to exchange. It's not a huge commitment, and the bonus is getting fabrics in your quilt that you don't have.

If you want to make the quilt on your own, you may want to use paper foundations for piecing the half-square-triangle units, or at least for the smaller ones. They finish at 1½" square, which is a bit on the small size for some. Using foundation patterns means you make several units at a time from the same pair of fabrics. In the end, you can scatter them around in various blocks, making for a lovely scrappy quilt.

Piecing for 1 Flock of Geese Block

The instructions below are for one block. Repeat as many times as needed to make the required number of blocks. Sew all pieces with right sides together using a ¼" seam allowance unless otherwise noted. Press the seam allowances as indicated by the arrows or as otherwise specified.

1. Select a set of pieces cut for one block. Use a pencil and an acrylic ruler to draw a diagonal sewing line from corner to corner on the wrong side of the cream 4" square. Layer the marked cream square on top of the brown 4" square with right sides together. Stitch ¼" from each side of the drawn line. Cut the stitched pair in half on the drawn line to yield two half-square-triangle units. Square the units to measure 3½" × 3½". Press.

Make 2 units,
3½" x 3½".

2. Draw an X from corner to corner on the wrong side of the cream 5½" square. Place the marked cream square on top of the red 5½" square with right sides together. Stitch ¼" from each side of *both* drawn lines.

Finished quilt size: 36½" × 36½" • **Finished block size:** 6" × 6"

Designed and pieced by Jo Morton.
Machine quilted by Maggi Honeyman.

3. Cut the sewn layers in half vertically first, then in half horizontally, as shown, to create four smaller squares. Cut each of the smaller squares apart on the drawn lines to make eight half-square-triangle units. Square each of the eight units to measure 2" × 2".

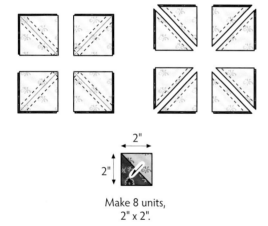

Make 8 units,
2" x 2".

4. Place four assorted red half-square-triangle units into a block arrangement, making sure all the red triangles face the same direction. Sew the blocks together in each row and then sew the rows together to make a unit that measures 3½" square. Press. Make two.

Make 2 units,
3½" x 3½".

5. Arrange two brown units from step 1 and two red units from step 4 in two rows of two units as shown. All the dark sides of the units should be pointing the same direction. Pin and then sew the units together in each row, matching the seam intersections. Sew the rows together. Referring to "Jo's Clipping Trick" on page 120, press the seam allowances toward the large half-square triangles to complete a Flock of Geese block that measures 6½" square, including seam allowances.

Flock of Geese block,
6½" x 6½"

6. Repeat steps 1–5 to make a total of 36 Flock of Geese blocks.

Pressing the Blocks

When joining the four units in each Flock of Geese block, nest the seams (and use the clipping trick at the center) to make assembling the quilt top easier. The photo below shows how I pressed each block.

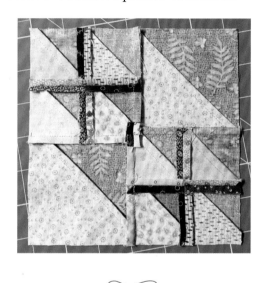

Assembling the Quilt Top

1. Referring to the quilt assembly diagram at right, lay out the 36 blocks in six rows of six blocks each. In the featured quilt, the brown and red triangles all point toward the center, which leaves a light outer edge. You may wish to change the directions of the blocks to achieve the opposite effect.

2. Assemble the quilt top in four quadrants of three blocks by three blocks as shown in the quilt assembly diagram. Pin and sew the top two quadrants together, matching the seam intersections. Repeat for the two bottom quadrants.

3. Pin the top and bottom halves together, matching the seam intersections. Join the halves, and press the seam allowances open. The finished quilt top should measure 36½" square.

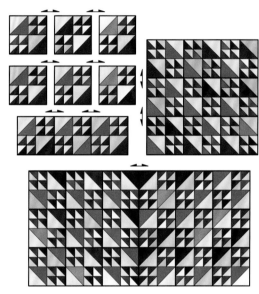

Quilt assembly

Completing the Quilt

Layer and baste the quilt top, batting, and backing. Quilt the layers. The featured quilt was machine quilted with an allover meandering design. Referring to "Jo's Single-Fold Binding" on page 126, or substituting your own method, use the binding strips to bind the quilt.

Ripples on the Pond

Jewel-toned prints and a generous sprinkling of triangle patchwork create a beautiful sense of movement in this striking quilt that's full of anytime charm. For seasonal appeal, consider choosing a theme such as harvest, patriotic, or yuletide, and create a quilt worthy of taking center stage.

~ Kim

SWAP TALK

The approach for this very scrappy block exchange is a little bit different from what's done in a typical swap, meaning that I structured this project so each participant contributes *two* Flock of Geese blocks to the quilt, with both blocks stitched from one dark (or medium) print and one light print. The benefit to this double swap is that the pieced blocks can be set into your quilt in such a way that the colors are spaced evenly and look intentional. Your finished quilt will have a beautiful balance, ensuring that no single "loud and proud" block becomes the focus of your quilt. For the final finishing touch to this project, a scrap of each medium or dark print is swapped with the pieced blocks, enabling the quilt center colors to be carried into the pieced border for added continuity.

Materials

Yardage is based on 42" of usable fabric width after prewashing and removing selvages. Chubby sixteenths are 9" × 10½".

32 chubby sixteenths of assorted medium and dark prints (collectively referred to as "dark") for blocks and borders

32 chubby sixteenths of assorted light prints for blocks and borders

⅜ yard of black print (or color of your choice) for binding

1¼ yards of fabric for backing

45" × 45" square of batting

Cutting

You'll need 64 Flock of Geese blocks to complete the featured quilt, with two blocks pieced from each chosen light and dark print combination. Cutting instructions are given for two blocks at a time; the number of pieces listed in parentheses provides the total amount needed to make 64 blocks. For greater ease in piecing the blocks, keep the pieces for each pair of blocks grouped together as you cut them.

CUTTING FOR 2 FLOCK OF GEESE BLOCKS

From *1* dark chubby sixteenth, cut:
1 rectangle, 3½" × 8½", to be included with block exchange
2 squares, 2⅞" × 2⅞" (combined total of 64)
8 squares, 1⅞" × 1⅞" (combined total of 256)

From *1* light chubby sixteenth, cut:
1 rectangle, 3½" × 8½", to be included with block exchange
2 squares, 2⅞" × 2⅞" (combined total of 64)
8 squares, 1⅞" × 1⅞" (combined total of 256)

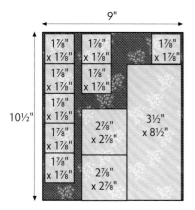

Cutting guide for chubby sixteenths

ADDITIONAL CUTTING TO COMPLETE THE QUILT

Cut all pieces across the width of the fabric in the order given unless otherwise noted.

From the 32 swapped dark 3½" × 8½" rectangles, cut a *combined total* of:
36 squares, 2⅞" × 2⅞"
72 squares, 1⅞" × 1⅞"

From the 32 swapped light 3½" × 8½" rectangles, cut a *combined total* of:
36 squares, 2⅞" × 2⅞"
72 squares, 1⅞" × 1⅞"
4 squares, 1½" × 1½"

From the black print for binding, cut:
4 strips, 2½" × 42" (For Kim's Chubby Binding method provided on page 127, reduce the strip width to 2".)

Finished quilt size: 38½" × 38½" • **Finished block size:** 4" × 4"

Designed by Kim Diehl. Pieced by Jennifer Martinez.
Machine quilted by Rebecca Silbaugh.

Piecing for 2
Flock of Geese Blocks

The steps that follow will make two blocks. Repeat to make 32 pairs of blocks (64 total). Sew all pieces with right sides together using a ¼" seam allowance unless otherwise noted. Press the seam allowances as indicated by the arrows or as otherwise specified.

1. Select a set of dark and light pieces cut for a pair of blocks. Use a pencil and an acrylic ruler to draw a diagonal sewing line from corner to corner on the wrong side of each light 2⅞" square and each light 1⅞" square.

2. Layer a prepared light 2⅞" square onto a dark 2⅞" square. Stitch ¼" out from each side of the drawn line. Cut the stitched squares in half on the drawn line to yield two half-square-triangle units. Press. Trim away the dog-ear points. Repeat with the remaining dark and light 2⅞" squares to make a total of four large half-square-triangle units measuring 2½" square, including the seam allowances.

Make 4 units,
2½" x 2½".

3. Repeat step 2, using the eight prepared 1⅞" light and dark squares, to make a total of 16 small half-square-triangle units measuring 1½" square, including the seam allowances.

Make 16 units,
1½" x 1½".

4. Lay out four small half-square-triangle units in two horizontal rows. Join the units in each row. Press. Join the rows. Press. Repeat to make a total of four small triangle units measuring 2½" square, including the seam allowances.

Make 4 units,
2½" x 2½".

5. Lay out two small triangle units and two large half-square-triangle units from step 2 in two horizontal rows. Join the units in each row; press. Join the rows. Press. Repeat to make a total of two Flock of Geese blocks measuring 4½" square, including seam allowances.

Make 2 matching Flock of Geese blocks,
4½" x 4½".

6. Repeat steps 1–5 to make a total of 64 Flock of Geese blocks.

Piecing the Quilt Center

1. Referring to the pictured quilt on page 61, lay out the blocks to form the quilt center.

2. Referring to the quilt assembly diagram on page 65, select four adjacent blocks, placing them in two horizontal rows of two blocks as shown. Join the blocks in each row. Press. Join the rows. Press. Repeat to make a total of 16 block units measuring 8½" square, including the seam allowances.

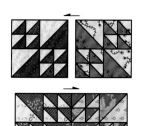

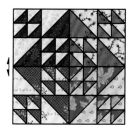

Make 16 units,
8½" x 8½".

3. Referring to the quilt assembly diagram on page 65, join four block units end to end. Press. Repeat to make a total of four block rows measuring 8½" × 32½", including the seam allowances.

4. Join the block rows to form the quilt center. Press the seam allowances open. The pieced quilt center should now measure 32½" square, including the seam allowances.

Four Times a Charm

For projects such as this Ripples on the Pond quilt, where the blocks are turned in different directions to form the design, I find that joining them in units of four blocks (rather than long rows) makes the assembly of the quilt center a breeze. Before I begin stitching the units, I take a moment to snap a photo of the layout with my smartphone, and then I refer to it as I stitch my patchwork. With these two steps it's easy to stay on track and make swift progress, because pieced block units are easier to work with than rows, and the finished positions of the prints and colors will be just as you intended.

Piecing and Adding the Inner Border

1. Referring to steps 1 and 2 of "Piecing for 2 Flock of Geese Blocks" on page 62, use the 36 dark and the 36 light 2⅞" squares to make 72 large half-square-triangle units.

2. Using the pictured quilt as a guide, lay out 16 pieced large half-square-triangle units end to end. Join the units. Press. Repeat to make a total of two side border rows measuring 2½" × 32½", including the seam allowances.

Make 2 side borders,
2½" x 32½".

3. Join the light edge of the pieced inner-border rows to the right and left sides of the quilt center. Press the seam allowances open.

4. Repeat step 2, using 18 pieced large half-square-triangle units, to make two additional pieced border rows. Join the light edge of these rows to the top and bottom of the quilt center. Press the seam allowances open. The pieced quilt top should measure 36½" square, including the seam allowances. (You'll have four leftover half-square-triangle units.)

Make 2 top/bottom borders,
2½" x 36½".

Piecing and Adding the Outer Border

1. Referring to steps 1 and 2 of "Piecing for 2 Flock of Geese Blocks," use the 72 dark and the 72 light 1⅞" squares to make 144 pieced small half-square-triangle units.

2. Lay out 36 pieced small half-square-triangle units end to end as shown. Join the units. Press the seam allowances open. Repeat to make a total of four pieced border rows measuring 1½" × 36½", including the seam allowances.

Make 4 borders, 1½" x 36½".

3. Referring to the quilt assembly diagram on page 65, join two of the border rows to the right and left sides of the quilt top. Press.

4. Join a light 1½" square to each end of the remaining two border rows. Press. Join these rows to the top and bottom edges of the quilt center. Press.

Make 2 borders, 1½" x 38½".

Completing the Quilt

Layer and baste the quilt top, batting, and backing. Quilt the layers. The featured quilt was machine quilted with the diagonal center seam of each block stitched in the ditch (along the seam line) and a repeating orange peel design stitched onto the patchwork. Referring to "Kim's Chubby Binding" method on page 127, or substituting your own favorite method, use the binding strips to bind the quilt.

Quilt assembly

Skipping Stones

There's an indefinable little *something* about strippy patchwork blocks that makes them incredibly homey, appealing, and inviting. Factor in the myriad design and setting options they bring to the table, and it's easy to understand why these blocks have been stitched and loved for generations.

~ Kim

SWAP TALK

To add a fun variation to the traditional Courthouse Steps block, I took my design one step further and added a row of checkerboard squares around the red center square. With this scrappy twist, the blocks are perfect for using up those last saved scraps of your favorite prints. As a speedy alternative, if you're piecing multiple identical blocks to be swapped, you can substitute strip sets for the checkerboard rows to streamline the patchwork process. For this approach, replace the top and bottom long rows of checkerboard squares with two strip sets, each consisting of four assorted print 1½" × 42" strips, and replace the short side rows of checkerboard squares with two strip sets, each consisting of two assorted print 1½" × 42" strips. Crosscut the pieced strip sets at 1½" intervals to yield 27 long or short checkerboard rows from each strip set. Repeat as needed to make the required number of blocks. This little shortcut for making many identical blocks is a great time-saver!

Materials

Yardage is based on 42" of usable fabric width after prewashing and removing selvages.

Approximately ⅓ yard *total* of assorted red print scraps for block center squares

Approximately 1 yard *total* of assorted medium or dark print scraps (collectively referred to as "dark") for block checkerboard squares*

Approximately 2½ yards *total* of assorted medium or dark print scraps (collectively referred to as "dark") for block rectangles

Approximately 2½ yards *total* of assorted light print scraps for block rectangles

⅝ yard of red print for binding

4 yards of fabric for backing

69" × 79" rectangle of batting

*See "Swap Talk" for a strip-set option to replace the individual checkerboard squares.

Cutting

You'll need 42 blocks to complete the featured quilt. Cutting instructions are given for one block at a time; the number of pieces listed in parentheses provides the total amount needed to make 42 blocks. For greater ease in piecing the blocks, keep the pieces for each block grouped together as you cut them.

CUTTING FOR 1 COURTHOUSE STEPS VARIATION BLOCK

From the assorted red scraps, cut:
1 square, 2½" × 2½" (combined total of 42)

From the assorted dark scraps for checkerboard rows, cut:
12 squares, 1½" × 1½" (combined total of 504)

From the assorted dark scraps for rectangles, cut:
A: 1 rectangle, 1½" × 4½" (combined total of 42)
B: 2 rectangles, 1½" × 6½" (combined total of 84)
C: 2 rectangles, 1½" × 8½" (combined total of 84)
D: 1 rectangle, 1½" × 10½" (combined total of 42)

From the assorted light scraps for rectangles, cut:
A: 1 rectangle, 1½" × 4½" (combined total of 42)
B: 2 rectangles, 1½" × 6½" (combined total of 84)
C: 2 rectangles, 1½" × 8½" (combined total of 84)
D: 1 rectangle, 1½" × 10½" (combined total of 42)

ADDITIONAL CUTTING TO COMPLETE THE QUILT

From the binding print, cut:
7 strips, 2½" × 42" (For Kim's Chubby Binding method provided on page 127, reduce the strip width to 2".)

Piecing for 1 Courthouse Steps Variation Block

The steps that follow will make one block. Repeat to make 42 blocks. Sew all pieces with right sides together using a ¼" seam allowance unless otherwise noted. Press the seam allowances as indicated by the arrows or as otherwise specified.

1. Join two assorted print 1½" squares. Press. Repeat to make a total of two pieced short checkerboard rows measuring 1½" × 2½", including the seam allowances. Join a pieced short row to the right and left sides of a red print 2½" square. Press. The pieced unit should measure 2½" × 4½", including the seam allowances.

Make 2 units,   Make 1 unit,
1½" x 2½".   2½" x 4½".

Seeing Red

As you begin piecing the checkerboard rows for your blocks, keep in mind that if you're including red prints (as I did), they'll work best when positioned in the end positions of the long top or bottom checkerboard rows. This placement will ensure they're not resting immediately next to the red center squares and will help keep your block design clearly defined.

Finished quilt size: 60½" × 70½" • **Finished block size:** 10" × 10"

Designed by Kim Diehl. Pieced by Connie Tabor and Kim Diehl.
Machine quilted by Connie Tabor.

2. Join four assorted print 1½" squares end to end. Press. Repeat to make a total of two pieced long checkerboard rows measuring 1½" × 4½", including the seam allowances. Join these long rows to the remaining sides of the step 1 unit. Press. The center-square unit should measure 4½" square, including the seam allowances.

Make 2 units,
1½" x 4½".

Make 1 unit,
4½" x 4½".

3. Join a dark print 1½" × 4½" rectangle to the left side of the center-square unit, and a light print 1½" × 4½" rectangle to the right side of the unit. Press.

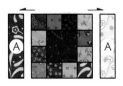

4. Join a dark 1½" × 6½" rectangle to the top edge of the block unit, and a light 1½" × 6½" rectangle to the bottom edge. Press.

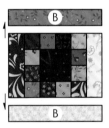

5. Continue stitching and pressing assorted light and dark rectangles to opposite sides of the unit as shown to complete a Courthouse Steps Variation block measuring 10½" square, including the seam allowances.

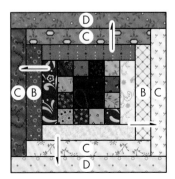

Courthouse Steps Variation block,
10½" x 10½"

6. Repeat steps 1–5 to make a total of 42 Courthouse Steps Variation blocks.

Piecing the Quilt Top

1. Referring to the quilt assembly diagram below, lay out the blocks in seven horizontal rows of six blocks, turning each block in the direction needed to form the quilt design.

2. Join the blocks in each row. Press. Join the rows. Press.

Completing the Quilt

Layer and baste the quilt top, batting, and backing. Quilt the layers. The featured quilt was machine quilted with an edge-to-edge design of repeating gentle S curves to soften the linear feel of the patchwork, with the length of the curves running vertically on the quilt. Referring to "Kim's Chubby Binding" method on page 127, or substituting your own favorite method, use the binding strips to bind the quilt.

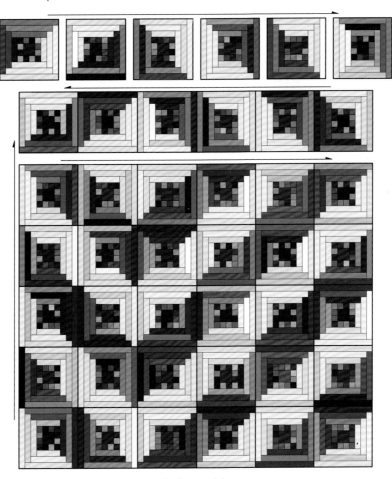

Quilt assembly

Courthouse Steps Variation Mini-Quilt

Finished quilt size: 10½" × 10½"

This sweet little mini is a great way to use up those saved scraps of favorite prints. Best of all, the small project size makes this quilt an easy finish!

Materials and Cutting

Assorted prints for block center:
4 squares, 1½" × 1½"

Assorted cream print scraps for blocks:
A: 4 rectangles, 1" × 2½"
B: 8 rectangles, 1" × 3½"
C: 8 rectangles, 1" × 4½"
D: 4 rectangles, 1" × 5½"

Assorted medium and dark prints for blocks:
48 squares, 1" × 1"
A: 4 rectangles, 1" × 2½"
B: 8 rectangles, 1" × 3½"
C: 8 rectangles, 1" × 4½"
D: 4 rectangles, 1" × 5½"

Assorted medium and dark print scraps for appliqués

Green print for stems:
1 square, 6" × 6"

Black print for binding:
2 strips, 2½" × 42" (For Kim's Chubby Binding method provided on page 127, reduce the width to 2".)

Backing:
1 fat quarter (18" × 21")

Batting:
1 square, 15" × 15"

Bias bar to make ¼"-wide stems
Liquid glue for fabric, water soluble and acid-free
Supplies for your favorite appliqué method

Piecing the Blocks

1. Referring to steps 1–5 of "Piecing for 1 Courthouse Steps Variation Block" on page 68, piece four mini blocks in alphabetical strip order. The blocks should measure 5½" square, including the seam allowances.

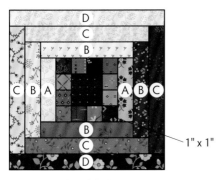

Make 4 blocks,
5½" x 5½".

2. Using the pictured quilt as a guide, lay out the blocks in two horizontal rows. Join the blocks in each row. Press the seam allowances in opposite directions. Join the rows. Press the seam allowances open. The quilt top should measure 10½" square.

Appliquéing the Mini-Quilt

1. Referring to "Making Bias-Tube Stems and Vines" on page 123, cut the 6" green square into four bias strips, 1" × 3½". Use the bias bar to prepare four stems. Apply a small amount of liquid fabric glue to the tip of the seam-allowance side of each stem, turn the raw end to the back of the stem approximately ¼", and use a hot, dry iron to heat-set and anchor the turned portion in place.

2. Using the patterns below, use your favorite appliqué method to prepare:

   ❀ 24 berries from assorted medium and dark print scraps

   ❀ 4 large leaves from assorted green print scraps

   ❀ 4 small leaves from assorted green print scraps

3. Referring to the pictured quilt, lay out one prepared stem, one large leaf, one small leaf, and six berries onto one corner of the quilt top. Use your favorite method to baste and stitch the appliqués in place, ensuring the raw end of the stem rests underneath a berry. Repeat on the remaining corners of the quilt top.

Completing the Mini-Quilt

Layer and baste the quilt top, batting, and backing. Quilt the layers as desired. I hand quilted the featured quilt in the ditch of each block (along the seam lines) and outlined the appliqués to emphasize their shapes. Use the black binding strip to bind the mini-quilt.

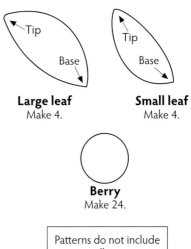

Large leaf
Make 4.

Small leaf
Make 4.

Berry
Make 24.

Patterns do not include
seam allowances.

At the Cabin

The beauty of a traditional Log Cabin quilt—where the blocks are half light and half dark, and divided along the diagonal—is that you have so many options for setting the blocks together. You can lay them out in diagonal stripes, which is referred to as Straight Furrows; in a central diamond pattern known as Barn Raising; or the option I chose, Sunshine and Shadows. For my quilt I chose a palette of rich browns and creams, but this design would work just as well in shades of blue, or even with a completely scrappy mix on the dark sides of the blocks.

~ Jo

SWAP TALK

❧ This quilt has 36 blocks; each finishes to 5½" square. Make it with five friends so that you will each make six sets of six blocks to exchange. Each participant will select his or her own pieced border or substitute a fabric border.

❧ Work first from your fabric collection. This approach lets you take advantage of yardage you already have. Even though the strips are 1" wide, you could consider using large prints, small prints, tonal, stripes, plaids, and dots to get a good play with your blocks.

❧ Be the same—but different! Kim used a Courthouse Steps variation of the Log Cabin block for her swap. I used the traditional Log Cabin block in my design.

Materials

Yardage is based on 42" of usable fabric width after prewashing and removing selvages. Fat quarters are 18" × 21" and fat eighths are 9" × 21".

Approximately 2 yards *total* of assorted light prints for blocks*

Approximately 2 yards *total* of assorted dark prints for blocks*

Fat eighth of rust print for block center squares

Fat quarter of plaid fabric for pieced border and cornerstones

½ yard of brown print for pieced border and single-fold binding

1⅓ yards of fabric for backing

45" × 45" square of batting

*Strips cut along the crosswise grain can be stretchy. To avoid blocks that stretch and wave, cut your strips from the more stable lengthwise grain (parallel to the selvages). To make sure you have enough fabric, gather pieces that have at least 18" of lengthwise grain.

Cutting

To make all 36 Log Cabin blocks for the featured quilt, I used approximately 28 light and 35 dark prints. Cut at least four lengthwise strips, 1" × 18", from each fabric to ensure you have a more than adequate number of strips (with some left over) to make the blocks.

Cutting for 1 Log Cabin Block

From the rust print, cut:
1 square, 2" × 2" (total of 36)

From the assorted lights, cut:
4 strips, 1" × 18" (total of 144)

From the assorted darks, cut:
4 strips, 1" × 18" (total of 144)

Additional Cutting to Complete the Quilt

Cut all pieces across the width of the fabric in the order given unless otherwise noted.

From the plaid fabric, cut:
6 squares, 6¾" × 6¾"
4 squares, 3¼" × 3¼"

From the brown print, cut:
3 strips, 3⅝" × 42", crosscut into 24 squares, 3⅝" × 3⅝"
4 strips, 1⅛" × 42"

Piecing for 1 Log Cabin Block

1. Follow the numbered strips in the block diagram and the sequence of colors below to make each Log Cabin block. Place each strip under the rust 2" square or pieced unit when sewing them together. It's important to use an accurate ¼"-wide seam allowance to make the blocks finish the same size.

Round 1:

Light prints for positions 1 and 2
Dark prints for positions 3 and 4

Round 2:

Light prints for positions 5 and 6
Dark prints for positions 7 and 8

Round 3:

Light prints for positions 9 and 10
Dark prints for positions 11 and 12

Round 4:

Light prints for positions 13 and 14
Dark prints for positions 15 and 16

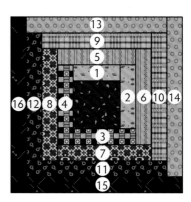

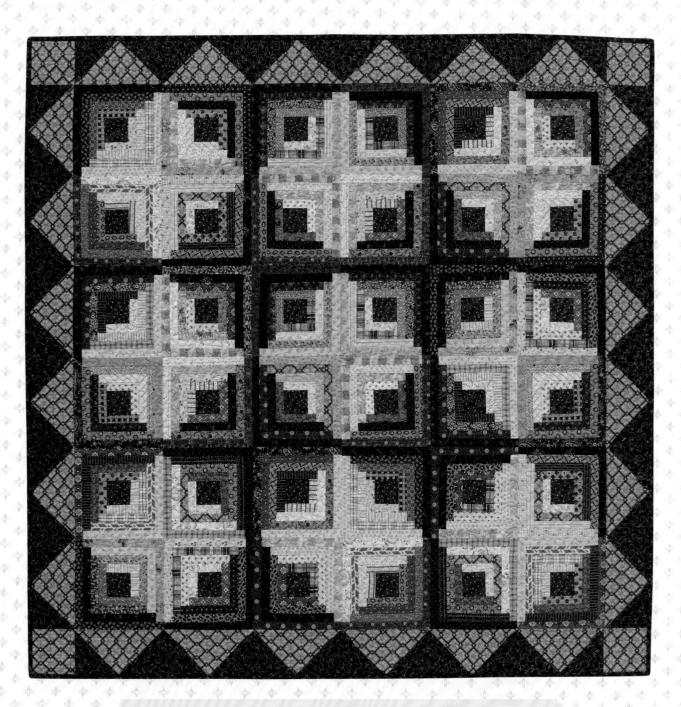

Finished quilt size: 39" × 39" • **Finished block size:** 5½" × 5½"

Designed and pieced by Jo Morton.
Machine quilted by Maggi Honeyman.

Organized Piecing

I placed my cut strips on a drying rack so they stayed nice and tidy while I pieced the blocks. The best part is that I could see everything I had chosen and made sure I included all the fabrics. I selected a different set of strips for each pair of blocks (I sewed two identical blocks at a time). To make sure I had a good balance in the quilt, I placed each block in the pair on the design wall as I finished them, well away from each other to make sure I didn't end up with identical blocks side by side. I also made sure there were some lighter strips on the dark side and some darker strips on the light side.

Refer to the quilt photo on page 77 for guidance, and have fun making this quilt!

2. Sew a rust 2" square to the light #1 strip, right sides together. Press the seam allowances away from the square. Using a rotary cutter and mat and an acrylic ruler, trim the gold strip ends even with the square.

3. Sew a second light strip, right sides together, to the right edge of the unit. Press the seam allowances away from the square. Trim the light strip ends even with the unit.

4. Sew a dark strip, right sides together, to the bottom edge of the unit. Press the seam allowances away from the square. Trim the dark strip ends even with the unit.

5. Sew a second dark strip, right sides together, to the left edge of the unit. Press the seam allowances away from the square. Trim the dark strip ends even with the unit. You have now added log-cabin strips to four sides

of the center square, completing round 1. Square the unit to 3" × 3".

Unit should measure
3" x 3".

6. Sew, trim, and press as before to add four more strips in clockwise rotation around the unit—two strips of a light print and two strips of a dark print. Square the unit to 4" × 4".

7. Continue to sew, trim, and press as before to add four more strips in clockwise rotation around the unit—two strips of a light print and two strips of a dark print. Square the unit to 5" × 5".

8. Continue to sew, trim, and press as before to add four more strips in clockwise rotation around the unit—two strips of a light print and two strips of a dark print. Square the unit to 6" × 6" to make a Log Cabin block.

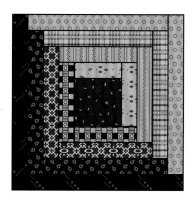

Log Cabin block,
6" x 6"

9. Repeat steps 1–8 to make a total of 36 Log Cabin blocks.

Trim in the Round

Trimming and squaring up after each round keeps your growing block exactly the right size. It evens out any excess so that you're not just trimming from the outer round of logs once you have sewn all four rounds (which would leave a scant outer frame).

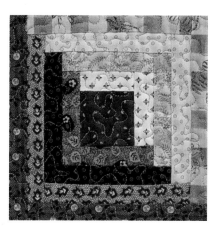

Front of block

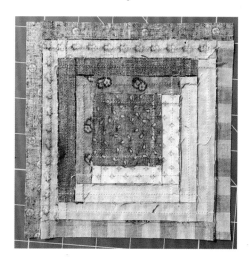

Back of block

2. Cut the unit apart on the drawn line. Press the seam allowances toward the smaller triangles, forming two square hearts.

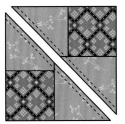 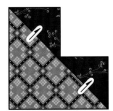

3. Position another marked dark brown 3⅝" square on the corner of the large triangle in one unit from step 2. Make sure the marked diagonal sewing line is pointing toward the center as shown. Sew with a scant ¼" seam allowance on both sides of the drawn line and cut apart on the line. Press the seam allowances toward the small triangles. Repeat with the second unit from step 2 to yield a total of four flying-geese units. Trim each unit to measure 3¼" × 6", including seam allowances.

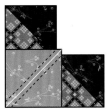 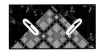

Make 4 units,
3¼" x 6".

4. Repeat steps 1–3 to make a total of 24 flying-geese units.

Making the Border Units

The pieced triangle border is made using what are called "no-waste" flying-geese units. The method produces four units at a time.

1. Using an acrylic ruler and a pencil, draw a diagonal line on the wrong side of the 24 dark brown 3⅝" squares. Align two marked squares on opposite corners of a plaid 6¾" square with right sides together. The dark brown squares will overlap in the center. Sew a scant ¼" seam on both sides of the drawn line.

 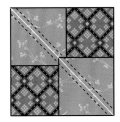

Assembling the Quilt Top

1. Sew the Log Cabin blocks into nine four-block units as shown, positioning the blocks so the light sides meet at the center. Press these seam allowances open. Make nine units measuring 11½" square, including the seam allowances.

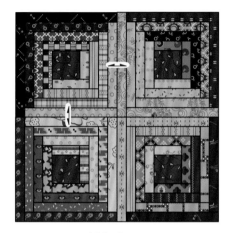

Make 9 units,
11½" x 11½".

2. Lay out the four-block units in three rows of three units each. Sew the units together in each row. Sew the rows together. The Log Cabin quilt center should measure 33½" square, including seam allowances.

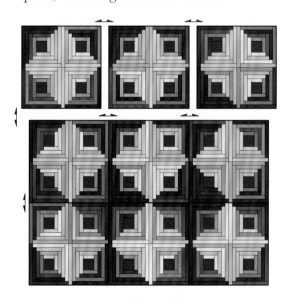

Quilt assembly

3. Join six flying-geese units side by side to make a border strip that measures 3¼" × 33½". Repeat to make four border strips. Sew a plaid 3¼" square to each end of two of the strips.

Make 2 borders,
3¼" x 33½".

Make 2 borders,
3¼" x 39".

4. Pin and then sew the two shorter border strips to opposite sides of the quilt top with the light triangles adjacent to the quilt top. Press the seam allowances open. Then pin and sew the longer strips to the top and bottom of the quilt in the same manner. Press the seam allowances open. The finished quilt top should measure 39" square.

Completing the Quilt

Layer and baste the quilt top, batting, and backing. Quilt the layers. The featured quilt is machine quilted with an allover meandering design. Referring to "Jo's Single-Fold Binding" technique on page 126 or substituting your own method, use the binding strips to bind the quilt.

My Christmas Goose

Capture the nostalgia of a vintage Christmas with this on-point quilt design. Envision it displayed on the wall behind a collection of Santas or holiday dishes set out on a sideboard. Or, enjoy relaxing with it in your favorite armchair. I used at least three different cream shirting prints in each block for a scrappy, vintage feel. If you happen to notice what seems to be a scorched area on one of the prints, it's actually spritzed with a walnut dye to subdue the whiteness. I didn't spray it evenly but decided to leave the block in the quilt to add to the vintage appeal.

~ Jo

SWAP TALK

Do you keep a scrap box? Goose Tracks is an opportunity to use up some small pieces of fabrics you've been saving. These blocks are not hard to make; they just have a few more pieces than some other blocks. I made this quilt with four friends, and we each created five sets of five blocks, for a total of 25. I kept Christmas in mind when selecting the colors. The brick reds and browns, shirtings, of course, and the pine sashing, say Christmas to me.

Materials

Yardage is based on 42" of usable fabric width after prewashing and removing selvages.

Approximately ½ yard *total* of assorted red prints for blocks

Approximately 1¾ yards *total* of assorted cream shirting prints for blocks (each block is pieced with three shirtings, labeled A, B, C)

Approximately 1 yard *total* of assorted brown prints for blocks

Assorted print scraps for block center squares

⅓ yard of red print A for cornerstones

1⅝ yards of pine green print for inner border and sashing

⅝ yard of medium brown print for setting triangles

1¾ yards of red print B for outer border

¼ yard of dark brown print for single-fold binding

3⅝ yards of fabric for backing

64" × 64" square of batting

Cutting

You'll need 25 Goose Tracks blocks to complete the quilt. Cutting is given for one block at a time for ease of having a block exchange; the number of pieces listed in parentheses provides the total amount needed to make 25 blocks. For greater ease in piecing the blocks, keep the pieces for each block grouped together. Each block contains one brown print, one red print, three shirting prints for the background, and a scrap fabric print for the center square.

CUTTING FOR 1 GOOSE TRACKS BLOCK

From 1 red print, cut:*
2 squares, 2½" × 2½"; cut each square in half diagonally *twice* to yield 8 triangles (combined total of 200)

From shirting print A, cut:
4 squares, 1¾" × 1¾" (total of 100)

From shirting print B, cut:
2 squares, 2½" × 2½"; cut each square in half diagonally *twice* to yield 8 triangles (combined total of 200)

From shirting print C, cut:
4 rectangles, 1¾" × 3" (total of 100)

From 1 brown print, cut:*
2 squares, 3⅜" × 3⅜"; cut each square in half diagonally *once* to yield 4 triangles (combined total of 100)

From 1 print scrap, cut:
1 square, 1¾" × 1¾" (total of 25)

*The majority of the blocks have brown "feet" with red "toes," but four of the blocks are reversed and require cutting 2 squares, 3⅜" × 3⅜", from a red print and 2 squares, 2½" × 2½", from a brown print for each block.

ADDITIONAL CUTTING TO COMPLETE THE QUILT

Cut all pieces across the width of the fabric in the order given unless otherwise noted.

From red print A, cut:
40 squares, 2½" × 2½"

From red print B, cut on the *lengthwise* grain:
2 strips, 3" × 52⅛"
2 strips, 3" × 57⅛"

From the pine green print, cut on the *lengthwise* grain:
2 strips, 3" × 47⅛"
2 strips, 3" × 52⅛"
64 strips, 2½" × 6¾"

From the medium brown print, cut:
3 squares, 11" × 11"; cut each square in half diagonally *twice* to yield 12 side setting triangles
2 squares, 6¼" × 6¼"; cut each square in half diagonally *once* to yield 4 corner triangles

From the dark brown print, cut:
6 strips, 1⅛" × 42"

Piecing for 1 Goose Tracks Block

The steps below are for one block. Repeat as many times as needed to make the required number of blocks. Sew all pieces with right sides together using a ¼" seam allowance unless otherwise noted. Press the seam allowances as indicated by the arrows or as otherwise specified.

1. Select a set of pieces cut for one block. Sew the long edge of a small red triangle to a shirting print A 1¾" square. Sew the long edge of a second small red triangle to an adjacent side of the cream square. Make four matching units.

Make 4.

Finished quilt size: 57⅛" × 57⅛" • **Finished block size:** 6¼" × 6¼"

Designed and pieced by Jo Morton.
Machine quilted by Maggi Honeyman.

seam allowances toward the light rectangles; press the clipped intersections open.

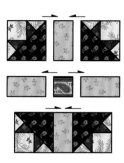 

Goose Tracks block,
6¾" x 6¾"

5. Repeat steps 1–4 to make a total of 25 Goose Tracks blocks (21 with brown feet and 4 with red feet).

2. Lay out two small shirting print B triangles and one unit from step 1 as shown. Sew the pieces together to make a pieced triangle unit. Make four matching units.

Make 4.

3. Sew a large brown triangle to a triangle unit from step 2 to make a corner unit measuring 3" square. Make four matching units.

Make 4 units,
3" x 3".

4. Lay out four matching corner units, four matching 1¾" × 3" shirting print C rectangles, and one print 1¾" square in three rows as shown. Sew the pieces together into rows. Join the rows to make a block that measures 6¾" square, including seam allowances. Use "Jo's Clipping Trick" (page 120) at the seam intersections to press the

Assembling the Quilt Top

1. Referring to the diagram on page 87, arrange the blocks, pine green 2½" sashing strips, red A 2½" cornerstones, and brown side and corner triangles in diagonal rows. Sew the quilt in three sections—the top-left corner, the bottom-right corner, and the long center row. Sew the pieces in each row together; press the seam allowances toward the sashing strips. Pin and then sew the sections together. Clip the seam intersections. Press the clipped intersections open and the seam allowances toward the sashing strips.

2. Press the quilt top carefully; do not stretch. Trim the quilt top along the outer edges to square up the quilt, leaving a ¼" seam allowance. The quilt center should measure 47⅛" square, including seam allowances.

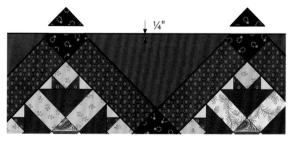

Trim, leaving a ¼" seam allowance.

3. Sew the pine green 3" × 47⅛" inner-border strips to the opposite sides of the quilt top and press. Join the pine green 3" × 52⅛" inner-border strips to the remaining sides of the quilt top and press. The quilt top with inner border should measure 52⅛" square, including seam allowances.

4. Sew the red B 3" × 52⅛" outer-border strips to the opposite sides of the quilt top and press. Join the red B 3" × 57⅛" outer-border strips to the remaining sides of the quilt top. The quilt top should measure 57⅛" square.

Completing the Quilt

Layer and baste the quilt top, batting, and backing. Quilt the layers. The featured quilt is machine quilted with a crosshatch diamond design. Referring to "Jo's Single-Fold Binding" technique on page 126, or substituting your own method, use the binding strips to bind the quilt.

Quilt assembly

Goose on the Loose

Merge elements from two time-honored blocks, and what's the happy result? A fetching take on the conventional Goose Tracks block, featuring an unexpected twist—a sweet little Churn Dash center! Full of drama, this scrappy quilt takes traditional patchwork to a whole new level.

~ Kim

SWAP TALK

For finished blocks with well-defined patchwork, I suggest choosing black prints with subtle texture and pairing them with prints in jewel-toned or high-contrast colors. Be a bit daring as you audition your prints, because one really enjoyable aspect of this project is to be surprised by the success of sometimes unexpected color combinations! Ask each participant to include a 2" × 3" scrap of print used for the Goose Tracks blocks as part of the block exchange, and you can incorporate these prints into the appliquéd leaf border for a subtle touch of added continuity.

Materials

Yardage is based on 42" of usable fabric width after prewashing and removing selvages. Fat quarters are 18" × 21".

25 assorted black print squares, 8" × 8" (approximately 1⅓ yards *total*), for block background

25 assorted print A squares, 7" × 7" (approximately 1⅛ yards *total*), for Goose Tracks portion of blocks

25 coordinating assorted print B rectangles, 4" × 7" (approximately ⅔ yard *total*), for Churn Dash portion of blocks

⅓ yard of black print #1 for sashing

⅝ yard of black print #2 for border

1 fat quarter of green print for vines

Approximately ⅓ yard *total* of assorted print scraps for leaf appliqués

⅜ yard of teal print for binding

1¼ yards of fabric for backing

44" × 44" square of batting

Bias bar to make ¼"-wide vines

1 sheet of freezer paper, approximately 8½" × 11"

Liquid glue for fabric, water soluble and acid-free

Supplies for your favorite appliqué method

Cutting

You'll need 25 Goose on the Loose blocks to complete the featured quilt, with each block using one assorted black print, one assorted print A, and one assorted print B. Cutting instructions are given for one block at a time; the number of pieces listed in parentheses provides the total amount needed to make 25 blocks. For greater ease in piecing, keep the pieces for each block grouped together as you cut them. Cutting instructions are provided separately for the leaf appliqués.

CUTTING FOR 1 GOOSE ON THE LOOSE BLOCK

From *1* black 8" square, cut:
1 rectangle, 2" × 7" (combined total of 25)
4 squares, 1⅞" × 1⅞" (combined total of 100); cut
   each square in half diagonally *once* to yield
   2 triangles (combined total of 200)
4 squares, 1½" × 1½" (combined total of 100)
1 rectangle, 2" × 3" (combined total of 25); set
   aside to be included with the block exchange

From *1* print A assorted 7" square, cut:
2 squares, 2⅞" × 2⅞" (combined total of 50); cut
   each square in half diagonally *once* to yield
   2 triangles (combined total of 100)

4 squares, 1⅞" × 1⅞" (combined total of 100); cut
   each square in half diagonally *once* to yield
   2 triangles (combined total of 200)
1 square, 1½" × 1½" (combined total of 25)

From *1* print B 4" × 7" rectangle, cut:
1 rectangle, 1" × 7" (combined total of 25)
4 squares, 1½" × 1½" (combined total of 100)

ADDITIONAL CUTTING TO COMPLETE THE QUILT

From black print #1, cut:
6 strips, 1½" × 42"; crosscut into:
   20 rectangles, 1½" × 5½"
   4 strips, 1½" × 29½"

From black print #2, cut:
4 strips, 4½" × 42"; crosscut into:
   2 strips, 4½" × 29½"
   2 strips, 4½" × 37½"

From the green print, cut:
Enough 1"-wide *bias* strips to make an
   approximate 156" length when sewn together
   end to end

From the teal print for binding, cut:
4 strips, 2½" × 42" (For Kim's Chubby Binding
   method provided on page 127, reduce the
   strip width to 2".)

Finished quilt size: 37½" × 37½" • **Finished block size:** 5" × 5"

Designed, pieced, and machine appliquéd by Kim Diehl.
Machine quilted by Rebecca Silbaugh.

the rows. Press. Repeat to make a total of four pieced units.

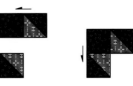

Make 4 units.

3. Layer a 2⅞" A triangle onto a pieced unit from step 2 as shown. Join the pieces along the long diagonal triangle edge, using a ¼" seam allowance. Trim away the excess portion of the half-square-triangle units extending beyond the top triangle. Press. Trim away the dog-ear points. Repeat to make a total of four corner units measuring 2½" square, including the seam allowances.

Make 4 corner units, 2½" x 2½".

Piecing for 1 Goose on the Loose Block

The instructions that follow will make one block. Repeat these steps to make 25 blocks. Sew all pieces with right sides together using a ¼" seam allowance unless otherwise noted. Press the seam allowances as indicated by the arrows or as otherwise specified.

1. Select a set of black, A print, and B print pieces cut for one block. Join a 1⅞" black and A triangle along the long diagonal edges. Press. Trim away the dog-ear points. Repeat to make a total of eight half-square-triangle units measuring 1½" square, including the seam allowances.

Make 8 units, 1½" x 1½".

2. Lay out two half-square-triangle units and one black 1½" square in two rows as shown. Join the pieces in the top row. Press. Join

4. Use a pencil and an acrylic ruler to draw a diagonal sewing line from corner to corner on the wrong side of each 1½" B square. Layer a prepared square onto a corner unit as shown. Stitch the pieces along the drawn diagonal line. Fold the resulting inner triangle open, aligning the corner with the corner of the unit underneath. Press. Trim away the layers beneath the top triangle, leaving a ¼" seam allowance. Repeat to make a total of four completed corner units measuring 2½" square, including the seam allowances.

Make 4 units, 2½" x 2½".

5. Join the black 2" × 7" rectangle and the 1" × 7" B rectangle along the long edges to make a strip set. Press. Crosscut the strip set at 1½" intervals to make four segments measuring 1½" × 2½", including the seam allowances.

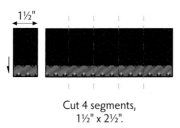

Cut 4 segments,
1½" x 2½".

6. Lay out the four corner units from step 4, four strip-set segments, and the 1½" A square in three horizontal rows as shown. Join the pieces in each row; press. Join the rows. Press. The Goose on the Loose block should measure 5½" square, including the seam allowances.

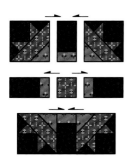 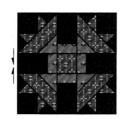

Goose on the Loose block,
5½" x 5½"

7. Repeat steps 1–6 to make a total of 25 Goose on the Loose blocks.

Piecing the Quilt Center

1. Lay out five blocks and four 1½" × 5½" black print rectangles in alternating positions. Join the pieces. Press. Repeat to make a total of five block rows measuring 5½" × 29½", including the seam allowances.

Make 5 block rows, 5½" x 29½".

Pressing Well for a Fine Finish

For patchwork projects with many pieces, I routinely add a quick pressing step to help ensure that the seam allowances of my finished quilt will lie smooth and flat. After positioning my completed block or unit next to the component I'll be joining it to, I quickly check for accuracy in size and make any needed adjustments.

Next, I lay the pieced block or unit *wrong side up* on my ironing board and give it a quick mist of Best Press (or you can set your iron to the steam setting). While the cloth is still damp I use a hot iron to press my work from the back and set the seams firmly in place, ensuring they're positioned in the correct direction with no wobbles. I continue slowly and methodically, working my way across the entire block or unit, and then flip it to the front and finish with one more quick press (misting again, if I feel it's needed).

When I'm pressing an individual block, I place an acrylic ruler on top of the front side of the block while it's still warm, add a weighted item (I use a sand-filled pincushion) to the ruler, and let everything rest until cool.

These pressing steps are easy to add to your routine and they result in a pieced quilt top with smooth, flat seams.

2. Using the pictured quilt on page 91 and the quilt assembly diagram below as a guide, lay out the five pieced block rows and four 1½" × 29½" black strips in alternating positions. Join the pieces. Press the seam allowances toward the black strips. The quilt center should now measure 29½" square, including the seam allowances.

Appliquéing the Border Strips

The large, medium, and small leaf patterns, as well as the vine guide, are provided on page 97. Guidelines for Kim's easy Invisible Machine-Appliqué method begin on page 120, or you can substitute your own favorite method.

1. Referring to "Making Bias-Tube Stems and Vines" on page 123, use the bias bar and 1"-wide bias strips of green print to stitch

and prepare two vines measuring 35" long and two vines measuring 43" long.

2. Fold the sheet of freezer paper in half crosswise, waxy sides together, and finger-press the center crease. Unfold the paper, align the crease with the straight edge of the vine guide, and trace the curved shape and center mark onto the dull, nonwaxy side of the paper. Refold the freezer paper and use a hot, dry iron to fuse the layers; use scissors to cut along the drawn curve and complete the vine guide.

3. Fold a 4½" × 29½" wide black print #2 border strip in half crosswise, right sides together; use a hot, dry iron to lightly press a center crease. Position the straight edge of the vine guide onto the raw edge of a border strip (with the right side of the fabric up), aligning the marked center of the guide with

Quilt assembly

the pressed center crease of the border. Use a pencil to trace the curve along the guide edge, working from the center of the border strip out to each side edge. Repeat to prepare a second 29½"-long strip and two 37½"-long strips.

4. Dot the drawn curved line of a prepared short border strip with liquid fabric glue at approximately ½" intervals. Center and affix a prepared 35" vine onto the glue-basted line, extending any excess length beyond each end of the border strip. Make two. Repeat with the 43" vines to prepare two long strips. Use your favorite appliqué method to stitch the vines in place. Trim away the excess vine lengths, leaving the edges flush with the edges of the border strips.

Make 4.

Marking Clearly Visible Designs on Black Prints

While designs marked with pencil will be visible on most black prints, the print on any given fabric can occasionally make it difficult to see traced lines. If this is the case with your black prints, I suggest substituting Clover's fine-line white marking pen for your pencil—this pen makes marks that are visible on nearly any dark print, and it will simplify the appliqué preparation steps.

5. Use your favorite appliqué method to cut and prepare a total of approximately 80 leaves in the large, medium, and small sizes from assorted print scraps. (Don't forget to include any prints exchanged with the blocks!) For the featured quilt, I began with approximately 60 large leaves, adding 10 each of the medium and small leaves to my mix; this enabled me to lay out the basic design for each border strip, and I was able to round out the design with additional leaves in the appropriate sizes as needed. My best advice for the additional number of leaves needed is to please yourself.

6. Using the pictured quilt as a guide, lay out the leaf design on each border vine strip. When you're pleased with the arrangement, baste and stitch the leaf appliqués of each border strip in place.

Joining the Border to the Quilt Center

Using the pictured quilt as a guide, join an appliquéd short border strip to the right and left side of the quilt center. Press the seam allowances toward the border strips. Join the appliquéd long border strips to the top and bottom edges of the quilt center. Press the seam allowances toward the borders.

Completing the Quilt

Layer and baste the quilt top, batting, and backing. Quilt the layers. The featured quilt was machine quilted with a nondirectional interlocking clamshell design for overall texture. Referring to "Kim's Chubby Binding" method on page 127, or substituting your own favorite method, use the binding strips to bind the quilt.

Vine guide

Center →

Large leaf
Make 60.

Medium leaf
Make 10.

Small leaf
Make 10.

Appliqué patterns do not
include seam allowances.

Best of Friends

In true sampler style, this quilt includes a little bit of everything—simply pieced blocks for instant gratification, slightly more challenging blocks for a sense of accomplishment when you nail the patchwork, and a sprinkling of colorful leaves and vines to let you dabble in appliqué. Happy stitching!

~ Kim

Materials

Yardage is based on 42" of usable fabric width after prewashing and removing selvages. Fat eighths are 9" × 21".

Approximately 2½ yards of assorted prints (including at least 4 red prints) for blocks, sashing, border, and appliqués (I used primarily medium and dark prints, with a small handful of light prints included for a good range of color.)

Approximately 1½ yards of assorted tan prints for blocks

1 fat eighth of dark green print for appliqué vines

½ yard of black print for binding

2⅔ yards of fabric for backing

48" × 49" piece of batting

Bias bar to make ⅜" vines

Liquid glue for fabric, water soluble and acid-free

Supplies for your favorite appliqué method

Cutting

The instructions that follow will produce all the blocks and units needed to make the quilt top; for added choices and versatility, you may wish to cut an extra handful of the small (1½") and large (2½") checkerboard squares used in the quilt center and border. Cut all pieces across the width of the fabric in the order given unless otherwise noted. For ease in piecing the quilt top, keep the pieces for each portion of the project grouped together as you cut them. Use your favorite appliqué method to cut the large, medium, and small leaf patterns provided on page 97.

CUTTING FOR 4 COURTHOUSE STEPS VARIATION BLOCKS

From *each* of 4 assorted red prints, cut:
1 square, 2½" × 2½" (combined total of 4)

From assorted prints, cut a *combined total* of:
48 squares, 1½" × 1½"
4 rectangles, 1½" × 4½"
8 rectangles, 1½" × 6½"
8 rectangles, 1½" × 8½"
4 rectangles, 1½" × 10½"
12 large leaves
12 medium leaves
12 small leaves

Continued on page 100

Continued from page 98

From assorted tan prints, cut a *combined total* of:
4 rectangles, 1½" × 4½"
8 rectangles, 1½" × 6½"
8 rectangles, 1½" × 8½"
4 rectangles, 1½" × 10½"

From the fat eighth of dark green print, cut:
Enough 1¼"-wide *bias* strips to make 2 lengths, 20" each, when sewn together end to end using straight, not diagonal, seams

Cutting for 1 Large Ohio Star Variation Block

From *1* black print, cut:
2 squares, 5¼" × 5¼"; cut each square in half diagonally *twice* to yield 4 triangles (total of 8)
1 square, 4½" × 4½"

From *1* medium or dark print, cut:
1 square, 5¼" × 5¼"; cut in half diagonally *twice* to yield 4 triangles
2 squares, 3⅞" × 3⅞"; cut each square in half diagonally *once* to yield 2 triangles (total of 4)

From assorted prints, cut a *combined total* of:
24 squares, 1⅞" × 1⅞"; cut each square in half diagonally *once* to yield 2 triangles (total of 48). Please note that only 1 triangle from each of the 24 prints will be used; if desired, you can reduce the number of squares to 12 and use each of the 24 resulting triangles for a slightly less scrappy look.

From *1* tan print, cut:
1 square, 5¼" × 5¼"; cut in half diagonally *twice* to yield 4 triangles
2 squares, 3⅞" × 3⅞"; cut each square in half diagonally *once* to yield 2 triangles (total of 4)
12 squares, 1⅞" × 1⅞"; cut each square in half diagonally *once* to yield 2 triangles (total of 24)
4 squares, 1½" × 1½"

Cutting for 1 Small Ohio Star Variation Block

From *1* black print, cut:
2 squares, 3¼" × 3¼"; cut each square in half diagonally *twice* to yield 4 triangles (total of 8)
1 square, 2½" × 2½"

From *1* medium print, cut:
1 square, 3¼" × 3¼"; cut in half diagonally *twice* to yield 4 triangles
4 squares, 2" × 2"

From *1* tan print, cut:
1 square, 3¼" × 3¼"; cut in half diagonally *twice* to yield 4 triangles
4 squares, 2½" × 2½"

Cutting for 2 Large Churn Dash Blocks

From *each of 2* assorted prints, cut:
4 rectangles, 1½" × 2½" (combined total of 8)
2 squares, 2⅞" × 2⅞" (combined total of 4)
1 square, 2½" × 2½" (combined total of 2)

From *each of 2* assorted tan prints, cut:
4 rectangles, 1½" × 2½" (combined total of 8)
2 squares, 2⅞" × 2⅞" (combined total of 4)

Cutting for 10 Small Churn Dash Blocks

From *each of 10* assorted prints, cut:
4 rectangles, 1" × 1½" (combined total of 40)
2 squares, 1⅞" × 1⅞" (combined total of 20)
1 square, 1½" × 1½" (combined total of 10)

From *each of 10* assorted tan prints, cut:
4 rectangles, 1" × 1½" (combined total of 40)
2 squares, 1⅞" × 1⅞" (combined total of 20)

Continued on page 102

Finished quilt size: 41½" × 42½"

Designed and machine appliquéd by Kim Diehl.
Pieced by Kim Diehl and Jennifer Martinez.
Machine quilted by Rebecca Silbaugh.

Continued from page 100

CUTTING FOR 12 FLOCK OF GEESE BLOCKS

From *each of 12* assorted prints, cut:
1 square, 2⅞" × 2⅞" (combined total of 12)
4 squares, 1⅞" × 1⅞" (combined total of 48)

From *each of 12* assorted tan prints, cut:
1 square, 2⅞" × 2⅞" (combined total of 12)
4 squares, 1⅞" × 1⅞" (combined total of 48)

CUTTING FOR 6 HEARTH AND HOME BLOCKS

From *each of 6* assorted prints, cut:
4 squares, 1⅞" × 1⅞" (combined total of 24); cut each square in half diagonally *once* to yield 2 triangles (combined total of 48)
8 squares, 1½" × 1½" (combined total of 48)

From *each of 6* assorted tan prints, cut:
4 squares, 1⅞" × 1⅞" (combined total of 24); cut each square in half diagonally *once* to yield 2 triangles (combined total of 48)
6 squares, 1½" × 1½" (combined total of 36)
1 rectangle, 1½" × 3½" (combined total of 6)

CUTTING FOR 6 GOOSE ON THE LOOSE VARIATION BLOCKS

From *each of 6* assorted prints (these will be print A for the piecing steps), cut:
4 squares, 1⅞" × 1⅞" (combined total of 24); cut each square in half diagonally *once* to yield 2 triangles (combined total of 48)
2 squares, 2⅞" × 2⅞" (combined total of 12); cut each square in half diagonally *once* to yield 2 triangles (combined total of 24)
1 square, 1½" × 1½" (combined total of 6)

From *each of 6* assorted coordinating prints (these will be print B for the piecing steps), cut:
1 rectangle, 1" × 7" (combined total of 6)
4 squares, 1½" × 1½" (combined total of 24)

From *each of 6* assorted tan prints, cut:
1 rectangle, 2" × 7" (combined total of 6)
4 squares, 1⅞" × 1⅞" (combined total of 24); cut each square in half diagonally *once* to yield 2 triangles (combined total of 48)
4 squares, 1½" × 1½" (combined total of 24)

CUTTING FOR CHECKERBOARD SASHING, BORDER, AND BINDING

From assorted prints, cut a *combined total* of:
172 squares, 1½" × 1½"

From assorted prints, cut a *combined total* of:
64 squares, 1½" × 1½"
63 squares, 2½" × 2½"

From the black print, cut:
5 strips, 2½" × 42" (For Kim's Chubby Binding method provided on page 127, reduce the strip width to 2".)

Piecing the Blocks

Sew all pieces with right sides together using a ¼" seam allowance unless otherwise noted. Press the seam allowances as indicated by the arrows or as otherwise specified.

1. Using the pieces for the Courthouse Steps Variation blocks, follow steps 1–5 of "Piecing for 1 Courthouse Steps Variation Block" on page 68 to sew a total of four blocks measuring 10½" square, including the seam allowances.

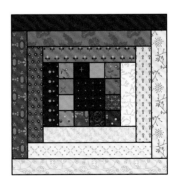

Courthouse Steps Variation.
Make 4 blocks, 10½" x 10½".

2. Using the pieces for the Large Ohio Star Variation block, follow steps 1–6 of "Piecing for 1 Ohio Star Variation Block" on page 32 to sew one block measuring 12½" square, including the seam allowances.

Large Ohio Star Variation.
Make 1 block, 12½" x 12½".

3. Using the sets of pieces for the Small Churn Dash blocks, follow steps 1–4 of "Piecing for 1 Churn Dash Block" on page 11 to sew 10 blocks measuring 3½" square, including the seam allowances.

Small Churn Dash.
Make 10 blocks, 3½" x 3½".

4. Using the sets of pieces for the Flock of Geese blocks, follow steps 1–5 of "Piecing for 2 Flock of Geese Blocks" on page 62 to sew 12 blocks measuring 4½" square, including the seam allowances.

Flock of Geese.
Make 12 blocks, 4½" x 4½".

5. Using the pieces for the Hearth and Home blocks, follow steps 1–7 of "Piecing for 1 Hearth and Home Block" on page 40 to sew six blocks measuring 5½" square, including the seam allowances.

Hearth and Home.
Make 6 blocks, 5½" x 5½".

6. Using the pieces for the Goose Tracks Variation blocks, follow steps 1–6 of "Piecing for 1 Goose on the Loose Block" on page 92 to sew six blocks measuring 5½" square, including the seam allowances.

Goose on the Loose.
Make 6 blocks, 5½" x 5½".

7. Substituting the larger-scale pieces for the Large Churn Dash blocks, follow steps 1–4 of "Piecing for 1 Churn Dash Block" on page 11 to sew two blocks measuring 6½" square, including the seam allowances.

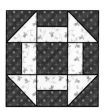

Large Churn Dash.
Make 2 blocks, 6½" x 6½".

top triangle, leaving a ¼" seam allowance. Repeat to make a total of four pieced corner units measuring 2½" square, including the seam allowances.

Make 4 units,
2½" x 2½".

10. Lay out the step 8 pieced hourglass units, the pieced corner units, and the black 2½" square in three horizontal rows. Join the pieces in each row. Press. Join the rows. Press. The pieced Small Ohio Star Variation block should measure 6½" square, including the seam allowances.

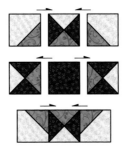 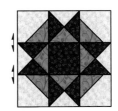

Small Ohio Star Variation.
Make 1 block, 6½" x 6½".

Assembling the Quilt Center

For easy assembly of this sampler project, the quilt blocks are joined into sections rather than into rows. The sections are then joined with checkerboard sashing and borders to complete the quilt top. As you assemble the quilt center, refer to the pictured quilt on page 101 as needed.

SECTION 1

1. For section 1, lay out the Courthouse Steps blocks in two horizontal rows of two blocks, with the dark portions of the blocks positioned in the outer corners. Join the blocks in each row. Press the seam allowances in opposite directions. Join the rows. Press the seam allowances open.

8. Using the pieces for the Small Ohio Star Variation block, lay out two black, one medium print, and one tan 3¼" triangle as shown. Join the triangles in each diagonal row. Press. Trim away the dog-ear points. Join the rows. Press. Trim away the dog-ear points. Repeat to make a total of four pieced hourglass units measuring 2½" square, including the seam allowances.

Make 4 units,
2½" x 2½".

9. Use a pencil and an acrylic ruler to draw a sewing line diagonally from corner to corner on the wrong side of each medium print 2" square. Layer a prepared square onto one corner of a tan 2½" square as shown. Stitch the pair together along the drawn line. Fold the resulting inner triangle open, aligning the corner with the corner of the tan square. Press. Trim away the layers beneath the

2. Choosing the prints randomly, join 20 assorted 1½" squares end to end to form a pieced checkerboard strip measuring 1½" × 20½". Press. Referring to the pictured quilt and the section 1 diagram below, join this pieced strip to the left edge of the unit from step 1 to complete the patchwork for section 1. Section 1 should measure 21½" × 20½", including the seam allowances.

3. Referring to "Making Bias-Tube Stems and Vines" on page 123, use the 1¼"-wide bias strips of dark green print to make two vines, each measuring 20" long. Using the section 1 diagram as a guide, lay out the vines on the light center to form the foundation of the appliqué design. Pin or baste the vines in place.

4. Using the pictured quilt as a guide, lay out four large leaves at the intersection of the vines. Position one large leaf at each vine tip, overlapping the raw end as needed to achieve the look you wish; trim away any vine length in excess of ¼". Lay out one large, three medium, and three small leaves along each vine as shown to complete the appliqué design (or create your own!). Pin or baste the leaves in place. Use your favorite appliqué method to stitch the vines and leaves in place. Section 1 is now complete.

Section 1
21½" x 20½"

Pressing Guidelines

Unless otherwise specified, I routinely pressed the seam allowances of all joined blocks open. When joining blocks or pieced units to checkerboard units, I consistently pressed the seam allowances toward the checkerboard units.

These quick guidelines will streamline the pressing steps as you assemble the quilt center.

SECTION 2

1. Join four Small Churn Dash blocks as shown to piece a unit measuring 6½" square, including the seam allowances. Press. Repeat to make a total of two small Churn Dash units; reserve one unit for section 5.

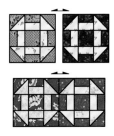 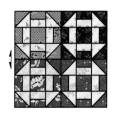

Make 2 units,
6½" x 6½".

2. Choosing the prints randomly, join 12 assorted 1½" squares end to end. Press in one direction. Repeat to make a total of three pieced checkerboard strips measuring 1½" × 12½", including the

seam allowances. Join a checkerboard strip to the right and left sides of the pieced Large Ohio Star Variation block. Press. The completed Large Ohio Star Variation block unit should measure 12½" × 14½", including the seam allowances. Reserve the remaining pieced 12½" checkerboard strip for step 3.

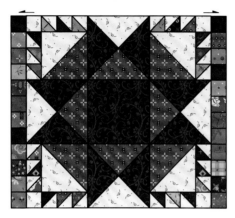

12½" x 14½"

3. Sew a Large Churn Dash block to the top edge of one Small Churn Dash unit from step 1. Press. Join the reserved checkerboard strip from step 2 to the left edge of the unit. Press. Join this unit to the left edge of the Large Ohio Star Variation block unit to complete the patchwork. Press. Section 2 should measure 12½" × 21½", including the seam allowances.

Section 2
12½" x 21½"

Section 3

Join eight pieced Flock of Geese blocks end to end to make a pieced row. Press. Choosing the prints randomly, join 32 assorted 1½" squares end to end to make a pieced checkerboard strip. Press. Join this pieced strip to the pieced Flock of Geese row as shown to complete the patchwork. Press. Section 3 should measure 5½" × 32½", including the seam allowances. Reserve the remaining pieced Flock of Geese blocks for section 6.

Section 3
5½" x 32½"

Section 4

1. Referring to the section 4 diagram on page 107, lay out four pieced Hearth and Home blocks (alternating the direction of the center tan rectangle every other block) and one pieced Goose on the Loose block; join the blocks to make a row. Press. Choosing the prints randomly, join five assorted 1½" squares end to end to make a pieced short checkerboard strip. Press. In the same manner, join and press 26 assorted 1½" squares to make a pieced long checkerboard strip. Join the pieced short checkerboard strip

to the right edge of the block row. Press. Sew the pieced long checkerboard strip to the bottom edge of the block row to complete the patchwork. Press. Section 4 should measure 6½" × 26½", including the seam allowances. Reserve the remaining pieced Hearth and Home and Goose on the Loose blocks for later use.

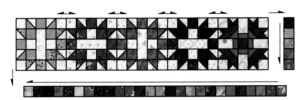

Section 4
6½" × 26½"

2. Sew section 2 to the bottom of section 1 as shown. Press. Sew section 3 to the right edge of this combined unit; press. Join section 4 to the top edge of the combined section to complete the patchwork. Press. The quilt center should now measure 26½" × 38½".

26½" × 38½"

Section 5

1. Join two Goose on the Loose blocks. Press. Join five assorted ½" squares end to end to make a short checkerboard strip. Press. Join this to one short end of the joined pair of blocks. Press. Join a third Goose on the Loose block to the checkerboard strip. Press. Join a 16-square checkerboard strip to the long right edge of the patchwork unit. Press.

Top

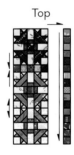

2. Join two small Churn Dash blocks. Press. Sew the reserved large Churn Dash block to the joined pair of blocks. Press. Join the reserved small Churn Dash unit to the large Churn Dash block. Press. Join six assorted 1½" squares to make a short checkerboard strip. Press. Join this strip to the small Churn Dash unit. Press. Sew the small Ohio Star Variation block to the small checkerboard strip. Press. Referring to the diagram on page 108, join step 1 and 2 units to complete

section 5. Press. Section 5 should measure 6½" × 38½", including the seam allowances.

Top

Section 5
6½" x 38½"

SECTION 6

1. Join the four reserved Flock of Geese blocks as shown. Sew 16 assorted 1½" squares end to end to make a long checkerboard strip. Press. Join this strip to the pieced blocks. Press. The top portion of the section 6 unit should measure 5½" × 16½", including seam allowances.

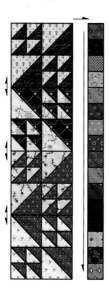

Top of section 6
5½" x 16½"

2. Sew and press two short checkerboard strips consisting of five squares each. Join a Hearth and Home block to opposite sides of one checkerboard strip. Repeat, sewing a Goose Tracks block to opposite sides of the second checkerboard strip. Join these two units as shown at right. Press. Sew this pieced unit to the bottom of the step 1 unit to complete the patchwork. Section 6 should measure 5½" × 38½", including the seam allowances.

Top

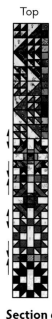

Section 6
5½" x 38½"

3. To complete the quilt center, join section 5 to the right edge of the quilt top. Press. Join section 6 to the left edge of the quilt top. Press. The quilt center should now measure 37½" × 38½", including the seam allowances.

Quilt center assembly

Piecing and Adding the Border

1. Choosing the prints randomly, lay out four assorted print 1½" squares in two horizontal rows. Join the squares in each row. Press. Join the rows. Press. Repeat to make a total of 15 four-patch units measuring 2½" square, including the seam allowances. Join and press two assorted 1½" squares to make a two-patch unit measuring 1½" × 2½", including the seam allowances. Repeat to make a total of two units.

Make 15 units, 2½" x 2½".　Make 2 units, 1½" x 2½".

2. Referring to the illustration, join 15 assorted 2½" squares and four four-patch units to make the right-hand border. Press. In the same manner, use 15 assorted 2½" squares and four four-patch units to make the left border. Using the pictured quilt on page 101 as a guide, join these pieced borders to the right and left sides of the quilt center. Press the seam allowances toward the border strips. The pieced quilt top should now measure 38½" × 41½", including the seam allowances.

Left border, 2½" x 38½"

Right border, 2½" x 38½"

3. Join 16 assorted 2½" squares, four four-patch units, and one two-patch unit to make a top border measuring 2½" × 41½". Press. Join 17 assorted 2½" squares, three four-patch units, and one two-patch unit to make the bottom border. Press. Join these borders to the top and bottom of the quilt center. Press the seam allowances toward the border strips.

Top border, 2½" x 41½"

Bottom border, 2½" x 41½"

Completing the Quilt

Layer and baste the quilt top, batting, and backing. Quilt the layers. The featured quilt was machine quilted with free-form echoing lines running vertically on the quilt to form a wood-grain design. Referring to "Kim's Chubby Binding" method on page 127, or substituting your own favorite method, use the binding strips to bind the quilt.

Harmony

It's hard to believe that there are any firsts left for me to attempt in patchwork, but here it is—my first quilt sampler that repeats blocks in four different sizes, the same blocks in the same sizes I've featured in all my previous quilts in this book. Combine Ohio Star, Wrench, Log Cabin, Flock of Geese, Hearth and Home, and Goose Tracks blocks, along with a row of four patches and two rows of flying geese. For some extra fun and movement, fussy cut sashing strips as I did!

~ Jo

Materials

Yardage is based on 42" of usable fabric width after prewashing and removing selvages.

Approximately 1⅜ yards *total* of assorted cream prints for blocks

Approximately 1⅜ yards *total* of assorted red prints for blocks

⅞ yard of red stripe for sashing*

¼ yard of red print for binding

⅞ yard of fabric for backing

27" × 33" rectangle of batting

*Look for a fabric with at least 6 repeats of a narrow stripe. The stripe should be approximately ½" wide.

Cutting

Cutting is given for one block at a time for ease of having a block exchange; the number of pieces in parentheses provides the total amount needed to make all the blocks for the sampler.

CUTTING FOR 1 HEARTH AND HOME BLOCK (MAKE 2.)

From assorted cream prints, cut:
1 rectangle, 1¾" × 4¼" (total of 2)
4 squares, 2¼" × 2¼" (total of 8)
6 squares, 1¾" × 1¾" (total of 12)

From assorted red prints, cut:
4 squares, 2¼" × 2¼" (total of 8)
8 squares, 1¾" × 1¾" (total of 16)

Continued on page 112

Sampler Block Sizes

I've made only two sampler quilts in my 38 years of quiltmaking, and both were made with blocks of uniform sizes. The Harmony quilt is a more unusual approach, melding six different blocks of four different sizes. I believe that most multiblock samplers combine blocks that are increments of each other, such as 3", 6", and 9", or 4", 8", and 12". This was not the hand I had dealt myself: I wanted to work with the same size blocks I'd made for the quilts in this book.

I started out by making two of each block and playing with them to see what might happen. What happened was that I ended up making more blocks and tossing in some additional elements to build a sampler I was happy with. The whole process really became quite a puzzle.

To make all the blocks work well and fit together smoothly, I ended up adding a checkerboard row and a narrow sashing between block rows. The sashing really did the trick. It's visually interesting, with its serpentine print (I do love fussy cutting!), and it helps each section of blocks really stand out on its own.

Long story short: this sampler quilt was all about the math, so I'm fortunate that I love math. And if you don't love math, that's fine too. Because it's all figured out for you.

Continued from page 110

CUTTING FOR 1 GOOSE TRACKS BLOCK (MAKE 2)

From assorted cream prints, cut:
4 squares, 1¾" × 1¾" (total of 8)
2 squares, 2½" × 2½"; cut each square in half diagonally *twice* to yield 8 triangles (total of 16)
4 rectangles, 1¾" × 3" (total of 8)

From assorted red prints, cut:
1 square, 1¾" × 1¾" (total of 2)
2 squares, 3⅜" × 3⅜"; cut each square in half diagonally *once* to yield 4 triangles (total of 8)
2 squares, 2½" × 2½"; cut each square in half diagonally *twice* to yield 8 triangles (total of 16)

CUTTING FOR 1 OHIO STAR BLOCK

From 1 cream print, cut:
1 square, 2½" × 2½"

From a second cream print, cut:
2 squares, 3¼" × 3¼"

From 1 red print, cut:
2 squares, 3¼" × 3¼"
4 squares, 2½" × 2½"

CUTTING FOR 1 FLOCK OF GEESE BLOCK (MAKE 2)

From assorted cream prints, cut:
1 square, 4" × 4" (total of 2)
4 squares, 2½" × 2½" (total of 8)

From assorted red prints, cut:
1 square, 4" × 4" (total of 2)
4 squares, 2½" × 2½" (total of 8)

Continued on page 114

Finished quilt size: 22½" × 28½"

Designed and pieced by Jo Morton.
Machine quilted by Maggi Honeyman.

CUTTING FOR FOUR-PATCH STRIP

From *1* cream print, cut:
22 squares, 1½" × 1½"

From *1* red print, cut:
22 squares, 1½" × 1½"

CUTTING FOR NO-WASTE FLYING-GEESE UNITS

From assorted cream prints, cut:
3 squares, 3¼" × 3¼"

From assorted red prints, cut:
12 squares, 1⅞" × 1⅞

CUTTING FOR SASHING AND BINDING

From the red stripe, fussy cut on the *lengthwise* grain:
6 strips, 1" × 27"; crosscut into:
    3 strips, 1" × 22½"
    3 strips, 1" × 13½"
    2 strips, 1" × 6¾"
    4 strips, 1" × 4½"

From the red print for binding, cut:
3 strips, 1⅛" × 42"

Piecing the Blocks

Use a scant ¼" seam throughout.

1. Referring to "Piecing for 1 Hearth and Home Block" on page 48, follow steps 1–3 to make two Hearth and Home blocks measuring 6¾" square, including the seam allowances.

Hearth and Home.
Make 2 blocks,
6¾" x 6¾".

Continued from page 112

CUTTING FOR 1 WRENCH BLOCK (MAKE 6)

From 1 cream print, cut:
2 squares, 2½" × 2½" (total of 12)
1 square, 1½" × 1½" (total of 6)
1 rectangle, 1¼" × 6" (total of 6)

From 1 red print, cut:
2 squares, 2½" × 2½" (total of 12)

From a second red print, cut:
1 rectangle, 1¼" × 6" (total of 6)

CUTTING FOR 1 LOG CABIN BLOCK (MAKE 4)

From a red print, cut:
1 square, 2" × 2" (total of 4)

From assorted cream prints, cut on the *lengthwise* grain:
4 strips, 1" × 18" (total of 16)

From assorted red prints, cut on the *lengthwise* grain:
4 strips, 1" × 18" (total of 16)

2. Referring to "Piecing for 1 Goose Tracks Block" on page 84, follow steps 1–4 to make two Goose Tracks blocks measuring 6¾" square, including the seam allowances.

Goose Tracks.
Make 2 blocks,
6¾" x 6¾".

3. Referring to "Piecing for 1 Ohio Star Block" on page 24, follow steps 1–4 to make one Ohio Star block measuring 6½" square, including the seam allowances.

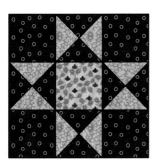

Ohio Star.
Make 1 block,
6½" x 6½".

4. Using the cream and red 4" squares, follow step 1 of "Piecing for 1 Flock of Geese Block" on page 54 to make large half-square-triangle units. Repeat with the cream and red 2½" squares to make small half-square-triangle units. Proceed with steps 4 and 5 on page 56 to finish a block. Make two Flock of Geese blocks.

Flock of Geese.
Make 2 blocks,
6½" x 6½".

5. Referring to "Piecing for 1 Wrench Block" on page 17, follow steps 1–3 to make six Wrench blocks measuring 4½" square, including the seam allowances.

Wrench.
Make 6 blocks, 4½" x 4½".

6. Referring to "Piecing for 1 Log Cabin Block" on page 76, follow steps 1–8 to make four Log Cabin blocks measuring 6" square, including the seam allowances. Substitute red print strips for the dark strips listed in the block instructions.

Log Cabin.
Make 4 blocks,
6" x 6".

8. To make the flying-geese units, draw a diagonal sewing line on the wrong side of the 12 red 1⅞" squares. Align two marked squares on opposite corners of a cream 3¼" square with right sides together. The squares will overlap in the center. Sew a scant ¼" seam on both sides of the drawn line.

9. Cut the units apart on the drawn line. Press seam allowances toward the smaller triangles, forming a square heart.

7. To make the four-patch units, lay out two cream 1½" squares and two red 1½" squares in two rows of two, as shown. Sew the squares together in each row. Join the rows to make a four-patch unit that measures 2½" square, including the seam allowances. Make 11 units.

Make 11 units,
2½" x 2½".

10. Place another marked red 1⅞" square on the corner of the large triangle in one unit from step 9. Make sure the diagonal sewing line is pointing toward the center as shown. Sew with a scant ¼" seam allowance on both sides of the drawn line and cut apart on the line. Press the seam allowances toward the small triangles. Repeat with the second unit from step 9 to yield a total of four flying-geese units. Trim the unit to measure 1½" × 2½".

Make 12 units,
1½" x 2½".

11. Repeat steps 8–10 to make a total of 12 flying-geese units. Join the units into two rows of six flying-geese units each.

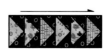

Make 2 units,
6½" x 2½".

Assembling the Quilt Top

Referring to the quilt assembly diagram at right, arrange the blocks on your design wall. Leave some space between the blocks for the sashing strips. Accuracy is very important when sewing this quilt, as there is no room to fudge. The quilt is assembled in sections. Press all seam allowances toward the sashing strips.

1. For section 1, join the four 6¾" square blocks (two Goose Tracks and two Hearth and Home) with two 6¾"-long sashing strips and one 13½"-long sashing strip. Section 1 should measure 13½" square, including the seam allowances.

2. For sections 2 and 3, join three Wrench blocks with two 4½"-long sashing strips in between. Sew a 13½"-long sashing strip to one long edge of each section. Both sections 2 and 3 should measure 4½" × 13½". Sew these sections to the top and bottom of section 1. The quilt top should now measure 13½" × 22½", including the seam allowances.

3. For section 4, join the 11 four-patch units in a row. Sew a 22½"-long sashing strip to the sides of this unit. It should measure 3½" × 22½", including the seam allowances.

4. For section 5, sew the Ohio Star block between the two flying-geese rows, and then sew a Flock of Geese block to the top and bottom, noting the orientation of the half-square-triangle units in the blocks. This section should measure 6½" × 22½", including the seam allowances.

5. Join section 4 to 5 and sew to the left edge of section 1-2-3. The section should now measure 22½" square.

6. To make section 6, join the four Log Cabin blocks in a row. Sew a 22½"-long sashing strip to the bottom edge of the column and then join this section to the top of the quilt. The completed quilt top should measure 22½" × 28½".

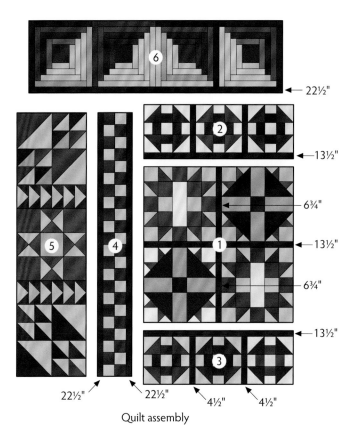

Quilt assembly

Completing the Quilt

Layer and baste the quilt top, batting, and backing. Quilt the layers. The featured quilt is quilted by machine in a smallish allover meander. Referring to "Jo's Single-Fold Binding" (page 126) or substituting your favorite method, join the red print strips into one length and use it to bind the quilt.

Guidelines for Block Exchanges

Once you've gathered a group of friends to exchange blocks, it's a good idea to establish some basic guidelines so everyone is on the same page and disappointments can be avoided. Agreeing on a few simple rules now will help ensure a successful swap. As a group:

❀ Determine which block you're going to exchange, and the finished size of the block (if you're going to vary from the size given in this book).

❀ Decide your color preferences for the exchange.

❀ Determine the total number of blocks each person will receive. Once the number of blocks has been decided upon, divide it by the number of participants to calculate the number of blocks that should be included in each swapped set. For instance, if the group feels that 30 blocks would make a nice-size quilt and you have five members in the group, divide 30 blocks by five participants for a total of six blocks. Each member will need to make five sets of six identical blocks, one set to keep and one set for each of the remaining group members. Always make an evenly divisible number of blocks; each person can make more if they wish.

❀ Decide whether fabrics should be prewashed or not. If prewashing is the chosen option, keep in mind that some participants may have allergies or be sensitive to fragrances; consider using fragrance-free soap or detergent and eliminating the use of fabric softener.

❀ Establish a realistic time frame for stitching the blocks, and set a due date. Keep in mind that if the block design is intricate or there are many blocks to be stitched, it will take longer to complete the sets.

❀ Appoint a "hostess" for the exchange. Having a hostess will help the swap run smoothly, because this person will make sure everyone receives a list of required materials and instructions for making the selected block. The hostess will also establish a deadline for the exchange of the blocks, receive the stitched blocks for distribution to the group members, and serve as the go-to person if anyone has questions along the way. In other words, the position of hostess is one of mega-importance!

❀ Set any additional guidelines to help ensure the participants enjoy a successful swap.

Jo and Kim's Quiltmaking Basics

This section provides how-to information for many of the techniques used to make the quilts included in this book. For even more details, please visit ShopMartingale.com/HowtoQuilt, where you can download free illustrated guidelines.

Cutting Bias Strips

Some projects in this book call for bias strips (lengths of cloth that have been cut diagonally rather than across the width of the fabric), which are usually used when a quilt features appliquéd stems and vines. The steps provided here describe Kim's preferred method for cutting these strips, as they enable her to work with a manageable size of fabric that produces strips approximately twice the cut length once they're unfolded. Another benefit of this method is that you can join the cut strips end to end to make one long strip, and then cut the exact lengths needed from this strip, resulting in little or no waste.

1. After pressing the fabric smooth, lay it in a single layer on a large cutting mat. Grasp one corner of the fabric and fold it back to form a layered triangle of any size you choose, aligning the top straight edge with the straight grain of the bottom layer of fabric.

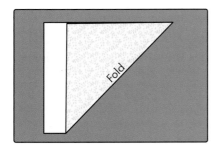

2. Rotate the folded fabric triangle to align the folded edge with a cutting line on your mat, ensuring the fold is resting evenly along the marked line to prevent a "dog-leg" curve in your strips after they've been cut and unfolded.

3. Use an acrylic ruler and rotary cutter to cut through the folded edge of the fabric a few inches from one pointed end. With the ruler aligned with the lines of your cutting mat, begin cutting strips at measured intervals from this edge (using the dimensions given in the project). If more strips are needed, simply begin again at step 1 and repeat the process, using another corner of your cloth or squaring up the end from which you've been cutting.

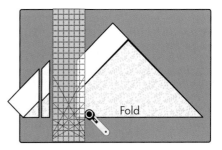

4. Square off the strip ends and trim them to the desired length, or sew multiple squared-off lengths together using straight, not diagonal, seams to achieve the length needed. Press the seam allowances to one side, all in the same direction. If you'll be using a bias bar to make bias-tube stems, joining the lengths with straight seams is best, because they allow the bias bar to slide

easily through the sewn tubes in the same direction the seams are resting in, and the bias bar won't get caught on the seams.

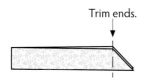

Trim ends.

Jo's Clipping Trick

This trick creates less bulk at the seam intersections of machine-stitched pieces, which will result in flatter blocks.

1. Clip the seam through both layers of the seam allowance ¼" from each side of the seam intersection (the clips will be ½" apart).

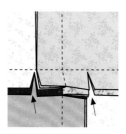

2. Press the clipped intersection open, and press the seam allowances in the direction they would like to lie.

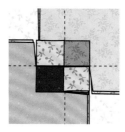

Kim's Invisible Machine-Appliqué Technique

The results that can be achieved with this technique are fantastic because they closely resemble the look of needle turn, but the process is much quicker. In addition to your standard quiltmaking supplies, you'll need the following tools and products:

❁ .004 monofilament thread in smoke and clear colors

❁ Awl or stiletto tool with a sharp point

❁ Bias bars in various widths

❁ Embroidery scissors with a fine, sharp point

❁ Freezer paper

❁ Iron with a pointed pressing tip (travel-sized irons work well for this technique)

❁ Liquid fabric glue, water soluble and acid-free (my favorite brand is Quilter's Choice Basting Glue by Beacon Adhesives)

❁ Open-toe presser foot

❁ Pressing board with a *firm* surface

❁ Sewing machine with adjustable tension control, capable of producing a tiny zigzag stitch

❁ Size 75/11 (or smaller) machine-quilting needles

❁ Tweezers with rounded tips

PREPARING PATTERN TEMPLATES

Tracing *around* a sturdy template to make the needed pattern pieces, rather than over the pattern sheet numerous times, speeds the appliqué process tremendously. Any time a template is used, only one will be needed, as it's simply a tracing tool. I recommend making templates from freezer paper (which eliminates the need to buy template plastic) using the steps that follow.

1. Cut a single piece of freezer paper about twice as large as your shape. Use a pencil to trace the pattern onto one end of the nonwaxy side of the paper. Fold the freezer paper in half, waxy sides together, and use a hot, dry iron (I place mine on the cotton setting) to fuse the folded paper layers together.

2. Cut out the shape on the drawn line, taking care to duplicate it accurately.

PREPARING PAPER PATTERN PIECES

Pattern *pieces* are the individual paper shapes that will be used to prepare the appliqués from cloth. Always cut pattern pieces on the drawn lines, as the seam allowances will be added later when the shapes are cut from fabric.

Use the prepared template (or pattern sheet, if you're preparing fewer than a dozen pieces) to trace the number of pattern pieces needed onto the nonwaxy side of a piece of freezer paper. To easily make multiple pattern pieces, stack the freezer paper (up to eight layers deep for simple shapes, and four to six layers deep for more complex shapes) with the waxy sides facing down; anchor the shape centers using pins to prevent shifting, or use staples at regular intervals slightly outside the shape in the background. Cut out the pattern pieces on the drawn lines and discard the background areas.

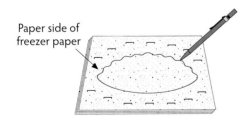

Paper side of freezer paper

To prepare mirror-image pieces, trace the pattern onto the nonwaxy side of one end of a strip of freezer paper, and then fold it accordion style in widths to fit your shape; anchor and cut the layers as previously described. When separated, every other shape will be a mirror image.

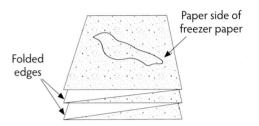

Paper side of freezer paper

Folded edges

PREPARING APPLIQUÉS

1. Apply a small amount of fabric glue stick to the center of the dull paper side of each pattern piece before affixing it to the *wrong* side of the fabric *shiny* side up, leaving approximately ½" between each shape for seam allowances.

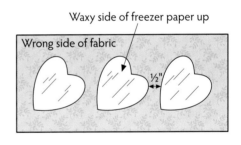

Waxy side of freezer paper up

Wrong side of fabric

½"

2. Using embroidery scissors, cut out each shape, adding an approximate ¼" seam allowance around the paper. For this technique, I've learned that more is actually better when it comes to seam allowances, as cutting too scant a seam allowance will make the fabric more difficult to work with. Any seam-allowance section that feels too bulky can be trimmed a bit, but you can't make scant seam allowances bigger.

When turning seam allowances to the back of an appliqué to press and finish the edges, it's actually better to leave the seam allowances of outer curves and points unclipped. The seam allowances of inner points or pronounced inner curves should be clipped once at the center position, stopping two or three threads away from the paper edge. If you're unsure whether an inner curve is pronounced enough to need a clip, try pressing it without one—if the fabric easily follows the shape of the curve and lies flat, you've eliminated a step!

Clip inner points
to paper edge.

PRESSING APPLIQUÉS

For the following steps, keep in mind that you'll want to work along the appliqué edge on the side that's farthest away from you, rotating the appliqué toward the point of your iron as you work in one direction from start to finish. Always begin pressing along a straight edge or a gentle curve, *never* at a point or a corner, because this will direct the seam allowance of any points toward your "smart" hand (which you'll later use to hold the awl or stiletto to fine-tune and finish any points).

1. Use the pad of your finger to smooth the fabric seam allowance over onto the waxy side of the pattern piece, following with the point of a hot, dry iron (I place my iron on the "cotton" setting) and *firmly* press it in place. To avoid puckered appliqué edges, always draw the seam allowances slightly backward toward the last section pressed,

letting the point of the iron rest on each newly pressed area as you draw the next section over and onto the pattern piece.

Direct seam allowance
toward center of shape.

2. For sharp outer points, press the seam allowance so the folded edge of the fabric extends beyond the first side of the pattern point. Fold over the seam allowance of the remaining side of the point and continue to complete the pressing. Apply a small amount of fabric glue stick to the bottom of the folded flap of fabric seam allowance at the point. Use the point of an awl or stiletto to drag the fabric in and away from the appliqué edge (not down from the point, as this will blunt it), and touch it with the point of a hot iron to fuse it in place. For narrow points, roll the seam allowances under slightly as you draw them in from the edge with the awl; this will enable the seams to be completely hidden from the front of the appliqué.

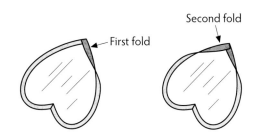

First fold

Second fold

3. To help achieve beautiful sharp appliqué points, ensure that your pressed seam allowance hugs the paper edge on both sides of any given point, as shown.

Wrong   Correct!

4. To prepare an inner point, stop pressing the seam allowance just shy of the center clipped section. Reaching under the appliqué at the clip, use the pad of your finger or the point of an awl to draw the clipped section of fabric snugly onto the paper, following immediately with the iron to fuse the cloth in place on the paper.

MAKING BIAS-TUBE STEMS AND VINES

To achieve finished stems and vines that can be curved flawlessly and don't require the seam allowances to be turned under, I use bias tubes. After cutting the strips specified in the project instructions (and referring to "Cutting Bias Strips" on page 119), prepare them as follows:

1. With *wrong* sides together, fold the strip in half lengthwise and stitch a scant ¼" from the long raw edges to form a tube. For

narrow stems, you'll likely need to trim the seam allowance to approximately ⅛" so it will be hidden from the front of the stem.

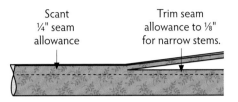

Scant ¼" seam allowance

Trim seam allowance to ⅛" for narrow stems.

2. Because of possible seam-allowance differences, the best bias-bar width for each project can vary from the size specified. Ultimately, you should choose a bar that will fit comfortably into the sewn tube, positioning the seam allowance so it's resting flat to one side (not open), and centered from side to side.

Bias bar

3. After removing the bias bar, place small dots of liquid basting glue at approximately ½" intervals underneath the layers of the pressed seam allowance. Use a hot, dry iron to heat set the glue and fuse the seam allowances in place.

BASTING APPLIQUÉS

Keep in mind as you lay out and baste your appliqués that there should be approximately ½" between the outermost appliqués and the raw edge of the background to preserve an intact margin of space around each piece.

1. Lay out the prepared appliqués on the background to ensure everything fits, remembering that any appliqué with a raw edge that will be overlapped by another piece should do so by approximately ¼".

2. Remove all but the bottommost appliqués, and then baste them in place. Glue basting is a great technique because there are no pins to stitch around, the appliqués won't shift, and the background cloth won't shrink during the stitching process.

To glue baste, fold over one half of a positioned shape to expose the back; place small dots of liquid basting glue along the fabric seam allowance (not the freezer-paper pattern piece) at approximately ½" intervals. Unfold and reposition the glue-basted portion of the appliqué, repeat with the remaining half of the shape, and use a hot, dry iron from the back of the unit to heat set the glue.

PREPARING YOUR SEWING MACHINE

As you prepare your sewing machine, be sure to match your monofilament thread to your appliqué, not the background, choosing the smoke color for medium and dark prints and clear for bright colors and pastels.

1. Use a size 75/11 (or smaller) machine-quilting needle in your sewing machine and thread it with monofilament.

2. Wind the bobbin with all-purpose, neutral-colored thread. I recommend avoiding pre-wound bobbins because they can sometimes make it difficult to achieve perfectly balanced tension.

   If your machine's bobbin case features a "finger" with a special eye for use with embroidery techniques, threading your bobbin thread through this opening will often provide additional tension control to perfectly regulate your stitches.

3. Program your sewing machine to the zigzag stitch, adjust the width and length to achieve a tiny stitch, as shown, and reduce the tension setting. For many sewing machines, a setting of 1 for width, length, and tension produces a perfect stitch.

〰〰〰〰〰〰〰〰〰〰〰〰〰

Approximate stitch size

STITCHING THE APPLIQUÉS

The following steps outline the stitching process for my invisible machine-appliqué technique. With a little practice, it's fun and easy!

1. Slide the basted appliqué under the presser foot from front to back to direct the threads behind the machine, positioning it to the left of the needle.

2. Beginning at a straight or gently curved edge, anchor the monofilament tail with your finger as your machine takes two or three stitches. Release the thread and continue zigzag stitching around your shape, with your inner stitches landing on the appliqué and your outer stitches piercing the background immediately next to the appliqué. After a short distance, carefully clip the monofilament tail close to the background.

3. Stitch at a slow to moderate speed, stopping and pivoting as often as needed to keep the edge of your shape feeding straight toward the needle.

   ❈ If dots of bobbin thread appear along the top surface edge of your appliqué as you stitch, further reduce the tension settings on your machine until they disappear.

   ❈ If the monofilament thread is visible underneath your appliqué from the back, or the stitches appear loose or loopy, increase the tension settings until they are secure.

4. For a secure inner appliqué point, stitch to the position where the inner stitch rests exactly on the inner appliqué point and stop. Pivot the piece and continue stitching.

Stop and pivot.   Continue stitching.

 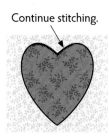

5. To secure an outer appliqué point, stitch to the position where the outer stitch lands exactly next to the appliqué point in the background and stop. Pivot the piece and continue stitching.

Stop and pivot.   Continue stitching.

6. As you complete the stitching, overlap the starting point by approximately ¼" and end with a locking stitch. If your machine doesn't have a locking stitch, extend the overlapped area to about ½" and the appliqué will remain secure.

STRING APPLIQUÉ

When two or more appliqués are placed closely together on the same layer, I recommend stitching your first appliqué as instructed in "Stitching the Appliqués" on page 124, but instead of clipping the threads when you finish a shape, lift the presser foot and slide the background to the next appliqué without lifting it from the sewing-machine surface. Lower the presser foot and resume stitching the next appliqué, remembering to end with a locking stitch or overlap your starting position by ¼" to ½". After the cluster of appliqués has been stitched, carefully clip the threads between each.

REMOVING PAPER PATTERN PIECES

On the wrong side of the stitched appliqué, use embroidery scissors to carefully pinch and cut through the fabric approximately ¼" inside the appliqué seam. Trim away the background fabric, leaving a generous ¼" seam allowance. Grasp the appliqué edge between the thumb and forefinger of one hand and grab the seam allowances immediately opposite with the other hand. Give a gentle but firm tug to free the paper edge. Next, use your fingertip to loosen the glue anchoring the pattern piece to the fabric; peel away and discard the paper. Any paper that remains in the appliqué corners can be pulled out with a pair of tweezers—if it's too small to see or easily grab, it's too small to worry about!

 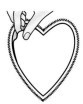

Binding

For information on traditional double-fold binding, visit ShopMartingale.com/HowtoQuilt. The information that follows summarizes Jo's and Kim's preferred binding methods.

Jo's Single-Fold Binding

Jo likes to use a single-fold binding, because she feels that double-fold binding is too heavy for most small quilts. To prevent the binding from stretching, she recommends using a walking foot or built-in dual-feed mechanism when attaching binding.

1. Cut 1⅛"-wide strips across the width of the fabric (selvage to selvage). Using a diagonal seam, join the short ends, right sides together, to make one long strip. Press the seam allowances open.

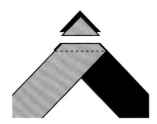

2. With right sides together, align a raw edge of the binding with the raw edge of the quilt. Beginning about 4" to 5" from the binding end, sew the binding to the quilt using a ¼" seam allowance. Stop sewing ¼" from the corner; backstitch and remove the quilt from the machine.

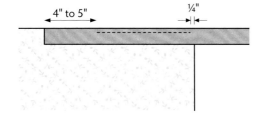

3. Rotate the quilt one quarter turn so you'll be ready to stitch the next side. Fold up the binding at a 90° angle.

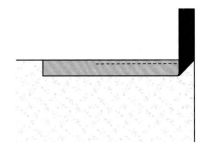

4. Next, fold the binding back down over the first fold and align the binding raw edge with the quilt raw edge. Reposition the quilt under the presser foot. Beginning with a backstitch, continue sewing the binding to the quilt top. Sew until you are ¼" from the next corner; backstitch. Repeat the folding and stitching steps at each corner.

5. Stop sewing about 5" or 6" from the start. Remove the quilt from the machine.

6. Fold the beginning of the binding strip toward the center of the quilt at a 90° angle. Repeat, folding the end of the binding strip toward the edge of the quilt at a 90° angle, leaving about a ⅛" gap between the folds. Press. By leaving the gap, the binding will lie nice and flat.

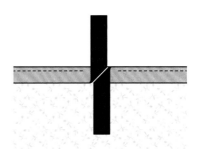

7. Align the fold lines, right sides together, and pin them in place. Sew on the fold line, backstitching at the beginning and end. Trim the excess binding strip, leaving a ¼" seam allowance. Press the seam allowances open. Finish sewing the binding in place.

8. Trim the batting and backing even with the quilt edges. Fold the binding over the quilt edge, turn under ¼", and pin it in place so it covers the first stitching, mitering the corners as you go when turning.

9. Blindstitch the binding by hand to the quilt back, using small, closely spaced stitches, and being careful not to stitch through to the front of the quilt. Take three or four stitches on the folds of the mitered corners to secure them.

Kim's Chubby Binding

Kim loves the look of "chubby" binding because it uses single-fold strips for less bulk and produces a wide strip of color to beautifully frame the back of the quilt. For this method you'll need a bias-tape maker to produce 1"-wide double-fold tape. As a matter of personal preference, Kim finishes most of her quilts using binding strips cut from the straight of grain, rather than the bias, because she feels this gives the quilt edges added stability and prevents stretching. For scrappy bindings, she loves the look when straight rather than diagonal seams are used.

1. Cut the strips 2" wide and join them end to end. Next, slide the pieced strip through the bias-tape maker *wrong side up,* pressing the folds with a hot, dry iron as they emerge. (Positioning the strip wrong side up will enable you to see the raw edges and ensure they meet in the center of the binding, because this will produce a uniform width on the back of the quilt.) As the tape maker slides along the pieced binding strip, the seam allowances will automatically be directed to one side as they're pressed, resulting in one less step!

2. Open the fold of the strip along the top edge only. Turn the beginning raw end under ½" and finger-press the fold. Starting along one side of the quilt top, not at a corner, align the unfolded raw edge of the binding with the raw edge of the quilt, and machine stitch the binding in place.

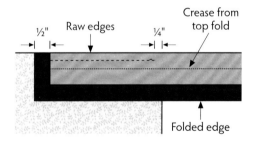

3. When you approach your starting point, cut the end to extend 1" beyond the beginning folded edge and complete the stitching.

4. Bring the wide folded edge of the binding over to the back and hand stitch it (including the mitered folds at the corners) using a small whipstitch. The raw ends of the strip will now be encased within the binding.

About the Authors

Kim Diehl

After falling in love with a sampler quilt pattern in the late 1990s, Kim impulsively purchased it, taught herself the steps needed to make it, and then realized she was smitten with quiltmaking. As her newfound passion blossomed into a full-time career, Kim began publishing her original designs, traveling nationally to teach her approachable quiltmaking methods, and ultimately designing fabrics . . . a dream come true for a girl who once wondered if she had what it took to make a single quilt!

Using modern time-saving techniques, such as the easy invisible machine-appliqué method she's known for, enables Kim to be prolific in her quiltmaking, and there's always something new in the works. Her very favorite quilts feature scrappy color schemes sewn from a mix of richly hued prints, and her designs often blend traditionally inspired patchwork with appliqué.

In addition to authoring numerous books, including her "Simple" series with Martingale, Kim continues to design quilting fabric collections and Simple Whatnots Club projects in her signature scrap-basket style for Henry Glass & Co.

After retiring from an extensive travel and teaching schedule, Kim now spends her days at home doing what she loves most—designing quilts and fabrics, baking, stitching, gardening, and being a nana to her grandchildren.

Jo Morton

Jo is a quiltmaker, fabric designer, teacher, author, and lecturer. Her use of color and design, as well as her fine stitchery, gives her quilts the feeling of having been made in the nineteenth century. Using an antique quilt as a source of inspiration, she creates a new interpretation. Her quilts complement both country and contemporary settings, and her work is included in private and public collections across the country.

In 1980 Jo took her first quilting class, and in 1985 she created her first "made to look old" quilt. She determined early on that if she ever hoped to make all the quilts she wanted to make, they would have to be small, and this size works perfectly in the small 1929 bungalow where she lives.

Jo is well known for her "Jo's Little Women Club" patterns, available through participating quilt shops since 2003. Her quilts have appeared in numerous magazines, and she's made several television appearances.

Jo lives in Nebraska City with her husband, Russ. Visit JoMortonQuilts.com to learn more, and follow Jo on Instagram at joquilts.